Quote Octopus
2/53 Barry Street,
Melbourne, Victoria, 3053
Australia
www.quoteoctopus.com

My mother was the most beautiful woman I ever saw. All I am I owe to my mother. I attribute all my success in life to the moral, intellectual and physical education I received from her.

George Washington

I think my mother is my biggest influence. There are so many things I hate about her but at the same time I'm thankful for her. All I know is that when I'm a parent I want to be just like my mom. I can talk to my mom more than any of my friends could talk to their parents.

Nikki Reed

Motherhood is a great honor and privilege, yet it is also synonymous with servanthood. Every day women are called upon to selflessly meet the needs of their families. Whether they are awake at night nursing a baby, spending their time and money on less-than-grateful teenagers, or preparing meals, moms continuously put others before themselves.

Charles Stanley

The natural state of motherhood is unselfishness. When you become a mother, you are no longer the center of your own universe. You relinquish that position to your children.

Jessica Lange

My mother had a great deal of trouble with me, but I think she enjoyed it.

Mark Twain

That strong mother doesn't tell her cub, Son, stay weak so the wolves can get you. She says, Toughen up, this is reality we are living in.

Lauryn Hill

My mother's wonderful. To me she's perfection.

Michael Jackson

The heart of a mother is a deep abyss at the bottom of which you will always find forgiveness.

Honore de Balzac

My mother said to me, 'If you are a soldier, you will become a general. If you are a monk, you will become the Pope.' Instead, I was a painter, and became Picasso.

Pablo Picasso

Only mothers can think of the future - because they give birth to it in their children.

Maxim Gorky

The mother-child relationship is paradoxical and, in a sense, tragic. It requires the most intense love on the mother's side, yet this very love must help the child grow away from the mother, and to become fully independent.

Erich Fromm

Having children is my greatest achievement. It was my saviour. It switched my focus from the outside to the inside. My children are gifts, they remind me of what's important.

Elle Macpherson

My mother taught me about the power of inspiration and courage, and she did it with a strength and a passion that I wish could be bottled.

Carly Fiorina

What greater aspiration and challenge are there for a

mother than the hope of raising a great son or daughter?

Rose Kennedy

Throughout my life, my mom has been the person that I've always looked up to.

Mike Krzyzewski

Men are what their mothers made them.

Ralph Waldo Emerson

I was raised by a single mother who made a way for me. She used to scrub floors as a domestic worker, put a cleaning rag in her pocketbook and ride the subways in Brooklyn so I would have food on the table. But she taught me as I walked her to the subway that life is about not where you start, but where you're going. That's family values.

Al Sharpton

When you are a mother, you are never really alone in your thoughts. A mother always has to think twice, once for herself and once for her child.

Sophia Loren

I don't want to let my life as a woman pass me by. There's a time to work, there's a time to be young and crazy, and there should be a time to enjoy motherhood. I'm actually looking forward to that.

Diane Kruger

My mother taught me to treat a lady respectfully.

Chris Brown

Motherhood is the greatest thing and the hardest thing.

Ricki Lake

My mother thinks I am the best. And I was raised to always believe what my mother tells me.

Diego Maradona

Do you know what you call those who use towels and never wash them, eat meals and never do the dishes, sit in rooms they never clean, and are entertained till they drop? If you have just answered, 'A house guest,' you're wrong because I have just described my kids.

Erma Bombeck

Completeness? Happiness? These words don't come close to describing my emotions. There truly is nothing I can say to capture what motherhood means to me, particularly given my medical history.

Anita Baker

When your mother asks, 'Do you want a piece of advice?' it is a mere formality. It doesn't matter if you answer yes or no. You're going to get it anyway.

Erma Bombeck

Mothers are all slightly insane.

J. D. Salinger

Yes, Mother. I can see you are flawed. You have not hidden it. That is your greatest gift to me.

Alice Walker

It's the moms of this nation - single, married, widowed - who really hold this country together. We're the mothers, we're the wives, we're the grandmothers, we're the big sisters, we're the little sisters, we're the daughters. You know it's true, don't you? You're the ones who always have to do a little more.

Ann Romney

When motherhood becomes the fruit of a deep yearning, not the result of ignorance or accident, its children will become the foundation of a new race.

Margaret Sanger

Morality and its victim, the mother - what a terrible picture! Is there indeed anything more terrible, more criminal, than our glorified sacred function of motherhood?

Emma Goldman

An ounce of mother is worth a pound of clergy.

Rudyard Kipling

A father may turn his back on his child, brothers and sisters may become inveterate enemies, husbands may desert their wives, wives their husbands. But a mother's love endures through all.

Washington Irving

I'm a Mommy's Girl - the strongest influence in my young life was my mom.

Susie Bright

I am sure that if the mothers of various nations could meet, there would be no more wars.

E. M. Forster

Mothers always find ways to fit in the work - but then when you're working, you feel that you should be spending time with your children and then when you're with your children, you're thinking about working.

Alice Hoffman

Motherhood is priced Of God, at price no man may dare To lessen or misunderstand.

Helen Hunt Jackson

The art of motherhood involves much silent, unobtrusive self-denial, an hourly devotion which finds no detail too minute.

Honore de Balzac

I ask people why they have deer heads on their walls. They always say because it's such a beautiful animal. There you go. I think my mother is attractive, but I have photographs of her.

Ellen DeGeneres

My mother used to tell me man gives the award, God gives the reward. I don't need another plaque.

Denzel Washington

It is not until you become a mother that your judgment slowly turns to compassion and understanding.

Erma Bombeck

I loved raising my kids. I loved the process, the dirt of it, the tears of it, the frustration of it, Christmas, Easter, birthdays, growth charts, pediatrician appointments. I loved all of it.

Jane Elliot

Sweater, n.: garment worn by child when its mother is feeling chilly.

Ambrose Bierce

Motherhood has a very humanizing effect. Everything gets reduced to essentials.

Meryl Streep

When you have a good mother and no father, God kind of sits in. It's not enough, but it helps.

Dick Gregory

The Vatican is against surrogate mothers. Good thing they didn't have that rule when Jesus was born.

Elayne Boosler

Mothers are the necessity of invention.

Bill Watterson

The fastest way to break the cycle of perfectionism and become a fearless mother is to give up the idea of doing it perfectly - indeed to embrace uncertainty and imperfection.

Arianna Huffington

Mothers are fonder than fathers of their children because they are more certain they are their own.

Aristotle

What is free time? I'm a single mother. My free moments are filled with loving my little girl.

Roma Downey

The mother's heart is the child's schoolroom.

Henry Ward Beecher

Take motherhood: nobody ever thought of putting it on a moral pedestal until some brash feminists pointed out, about a century ago, that the pay is lousy and the career ladder nonexistent.

Barbara Ehrenreich

The woman is uniformly sacrificed to the wife and mother.

Elizabeth Cady Stanton

Only God Himself fully appreciates the influence of a Christian mother in the molding of character in her children.

Billy Graham

I can only hope to be 10 percent of the mom mine was to me. She encouraged me to be confident and enjoy life. That's what I want for my son.

Charlize Theron

My mother taught me that we all have the power to achieve our dreams. What I lacked was the courage.

Clay Aiken

My mother told me on several different occasions that she was livin' her dream vicariously through me. She once said that I was getting' to do all the things that she would have wanted to have done.

Buck Owens

Who in their infinite wisdom decreed that Little League uniforms be white? Certainly not a mother.

Erma Bombeck

Being a mother is hard and it wasn't a subject I ever studied.

Ruby Wax

I stand fearlessly for small dogs, the American Flag, motherhood and the Bible. That's why people love me.

Art Linkletter

Motherhood is the strangest thing, it can be like being one's own Trojan horse.

Rebecca West

I was a brownie for a day. My mom made me stop. She didn't want me to conform.

Sandra Bullock

Just as a mother finds pleasure in taking her little child on her lap, there to feed and caress him, in like manner our loving God shows His fondness for His beloved souls who have given themselves entirely to Him and have placed all their hope in His goodness.

Alphonsus Liguori

I am truly my mother's son.

David Geffen

Mother is far too clever to understand anything she does not like.

Arnold Bennett

What do girls do who haven't any mothers to help them through their troubles?

Louisa May Alcott

Motherhood is the only thing in my life that I've really known for sure is something I wanted to do.

Cynthia Nixon

Tired mothers find that spanking takes less time than reasoning and penetrates sooner to the seat of the memory.

Will Durant

Motherhood is a dream. It really is absolutely amazing.

Jessica Simpson

Why do grandparents and grandchildren get along so well?
The mother.

Claudette Colbert

I think while all mothers deal with feelings of guilt,
working mothers are plagued by guilt on steroids!

Arianna Huffington

I believe that at least 70 percent of parenting goes to the
mother. In our house, I'm the one who knows about all the
school stuff, helps with the homework, organizes the play
dates, and remembers the birthday parties.

Cindy Crawford

Motherhood is at its best when the tender chords of
sympathy have been touched.

Paul Harris

How simple a thing it seems to me that to know ourselves
as we are, we must know our mothers names.

Alice Walker

It is only in the act of nursing that a woman realizes her motherhood in visible and tangible fashion; it is a joy of every moment.

Honore de Balzac

If there were no schools to take the children away from home part of the time, the insane asylums would be filled with mothers.

E. W. Howe

There are only two things a child will share willingly; communicable diseases and its mother's age.

Benjamin Spock

Of all the roles I've played, none has been as fulfilling as being a mother.

Annette Funicello

Every man must define his identity against his mother. If he does not, he just falls back into her and is swallowed up.

Camille Paglia

My mother was a personal friend of God's. They had ongoing conversations.

Della Reese

Mothers and children are human beings, and they will sometimes do the wrong thing.

Maurice Sendak

I sing seriously to my mom on the phone. To put her to sleep, I have to sing 'Maria' from West Side Story. When I hear her snoring, I hang up.

Adam Sandler

I may be the only mother in America who knows exactly what their child is up to all the time.

Barbara Bush

I owe much to mother. She had an expert's understanding, but also approached art emotionally.

David Rockefeller

I basically became a cheerleader because I had a very strict mom. That was my way of being a bad girl.

Sandra Bullock

A mother who is obsessing about being thin and dieting and exercising is not going to be a very good mother.

Jane Fonda

Everyone checks out my mom. My mom's hot.

Ashley Scott

I wish my mother had left me something about how she felt growing up. I wish my grandmother had done the same. I wanted my girls to know me.

Carol Burnett

The real menace in dealing with a five-year-old is that in no time at all you begin to sound like a five-year-old.

Jean Kerr

I'm so happy and thankful I made it a point be a stay-at-home mom.

Candace Cameron Bure

I'm sure that my mom would have been happy with any path I chose.

Joely Fisher

Mommy smoked but she didn't want us to. She saw smoke coming out of the barn one time, so we got whipped.

Loretta Lynn

Clearly, society has a tremendous stake in insisting on a woman's natural fitness for the career of mother: the alternatives are all too expensive.

Ann Oakley

I want to be more successful as a mother than I am in show business.

Celine Dion

A woman must combine the role of mother, wife and

politician.

Emma Bonino

Mothers don't let your daughters grow up to be models
unless you're present.

Janice Dickinson

My parents, especially my mother, were no influence on
me whatsoever.

Andy Partridge

My sisters and mom raised me to respect women and open
doors for them.

Milo Ventimiglia

I want to be a cool mom.

Tori Spelling

I'd lose my mind if I heard my kid call the nanny Mommy.

Toni Braxton

The man in our society is the breadwinner; the woman has enough to do as the homemaker, wife and mother.

Dorothy Fields

My mother gets all mad at me if I stay in a hotel. I'm 31-years-old, and I don't want to sleep on a sleeping bag down in the basement. It's humiliating.

Ben Affleck

I wanted to escape so badly. But of course I knew I couldn't just give up and leave school. It was only when I heard my mom's voice that I came out of my hiding place.

Zhang Ziyi

My mother worked in factories, worked as a domestic, worked in a restaurant, always had a second job.

Ed Bradley

What motivated me? My mother. My mother was an immigrant woman, a peasant woman, struggled all her life, worked in the garment center.

Al Lewis

My mom taught us the Serenity Prayer at a young age.

Toby Keith

I auditioned on my own. I tried to make a mark for myself without anybody's help, not even Mom's.

Kate Hudson

I am no mother, and I won't be one.

Brigitte Bardot

I guess I was a mom so late in life, my daughter was the greatest thing since sliced bread.

Candice Bergen

Always it gave me a pang that my children had no lawful claim to a name.

Harriet Ann Jacobs

My mother thinks I could have even run a larger company.

Christie Hefner

If my mom reads that I'm grammatically incorrect I'll have hell to pay.

Larisa Oleynik

Giving birth was easier than having a tattoo.

Nicole Appleton

One of the greatest titles in the world is parent, and one of the biggest blessings in the world is to have parents to call mom and dad.

Jim DeMint

Most of us have fond memories of food from our childhood. Whether it was our mom's homemade lasagna or a memorable chocolate birthday cake, food has a way of transporting us back to the past.

Homaro Cantu

Mom and Dad were married 64 years. And if you wondered what their secret was, you could have asked the local florist - because every day Dad gave Mom a rose, which he put on her bedside table. That's how she found out what happened on the day my father died - she went looking for him because that morning, there was no rose.

Mitt Romney

And the greatest lesson that mom ever taught me though was this one. She told me there would be times in your life when you have to choose between being loved and being respected. Now she said to always pick being respected.

Chris Christie

There's been times when I've had heartbreaking moments and I'm like, 'I can't believe you said that,' or 'I can't believe you did that'. And it hurts, it still hurts, and it'll always hurt, but I've never had somebody that I truly cared about just walk out on me, whether it was a boyfriend, or an aunt, mom or dad.

Shailene Woodley

My mom worked at McDonald's, and she decided she wanted to make more money, so she got into the management program at McDonald's. And that's how you move up the chain. It's not by demanding that minimum wage is raised; it's by actually acquiring the skills. That's the way that people get ahead in life.

Raul Labrador

My mom didn't let me play video games growing up, so

now I do. Gaming gives me a chance to just let go, blow somebody up and fight somebody from another dimension. It's all escapism.

Wayne Brady

Don't let people disrespect you. My mom says don't open the door to the devil. Surround yourself with positive people.

Cuba Gooding, Jr.

Good food and a warm kitchen are what makes a house a home. I always tried to make my home like my mother's, because Mom was magnificent at stretching a buck when it came to decorating and food. Like a true Italian, she valued beautification in every area of her life, and I try to do the same.

Rachael Ray

We need somebody who's got the heart, the empathy, to recognize what it's like to be a young teenage mom, the empathy to understand what it's like to be poor or African-American or gay or disabled or old - and that's the criterion by which I'll be selecting my judges.

Barack Obama

I was living as a young single mom. I was 19 when I was divorced, and my daughter was a year old, and I waited tables here three to four nights a week for several years while I was trying to support myself and my daughter and the day I got that acceptance at Harvard Law School was an unforgettable day.

Wendy Davis

When my wife and I met, I couldn't talk to her - and my defense mechanism is sarcasm. I belittle someone with verbal pokes and prods. I did it to her out of complete awe. When friends introduced us, I said 'Hi' - and turned my back. Later, I called my mom and best friend and said, 'I think I just met my wife.'

Mike Vogel

I have many valentines. My mom and my sister and my directors. I got calls from all of them. And my friends. I respect what Valentine's Day stands for because it is about love.

Michelle Trachtenberg

My mom always said that there would be haters. Not everyone can love ya.

Joel Madden

AIDS can destroy a family if you let it, but luckily for my sister and me, Mom taught us to keep going. Don't give up, be proud of who you are, and never feel sorry for yourself.

Ryan White

When I was growing up, my mother was always a friend to my siblings and me (in addition to being all the other things a mom is), and I was always grateful for that because I knew she was someone I could talk to and joke with, and argue with and that nothing would ever harm that friendship.

Marlo Thomas

I think my mom put it best. She said, 'Little girls soften their daddy's hearts.'

Paul Walker

When I was young and it was someone's birthday, I didn't have the money to buy nice presents so I would take my mom's camera and make a movie parody for whoever's birthday it was. When I'd show it them, they'd die laughing. That reaction was a high for me, and I loved that feeling.

David Henrie

My mom taught me the power of love. I learned to focus on the long-term big picture from my father. His sense of humor and light-hearted approach always make me smile. My husband is a pivotal anchor in my life. His influence encourages me to be independent and take risks.

Padmasree Warrior

There was the time I bought three cars in the span of three or four weeks. It was crazy; it wasn't greedy. It was mine, my girl's, my mom's. I got Benzes for my ladies. But I felt crazy. You have to understand I come from a world where we're very modest. But that's not greedy. That's nice, right?

J. Cole

My mom was a teacher - I have the greatest respect for the profession - we need great teachers - not poor or mediocre ones.

Condoleezza Rice

I don't want to be perfect, but I do want to be a role model. My mom always tells me that imperfections equal beauty. All of us are imperfect.

Miley Cyrus

You know, I don't think any mother aims to be a single mom. I didn't wish for that, but it happened.

Charlize Theron

My parents couldn't give me a whole lot of financial support, but they gave me good genes. My dad is a handsome son-of-a-gun, and my mom is beautiful. And I've definitely been the lucky recipient. So, thank you, Mom and Dad.

Ashton Kutcher

I was always going to church with my mom, dad and sister. I was literally raised under the godly influence both at home and church. There was no alcohol and no smoking at our house. That was the way a Bowden was supposed to live. My dad always told me to represent the Bowden name in a respectful manner.

Bobby Bowden

My mom keeps me going, man. She deserves such a good life. I just wanna give it to her. My dad, too. My family, my friends, they keep me motivated. Just knowing my personal legend, just knowing what I'm supposed to do, that keeps me going.

Big Sean

Did Superman really want to save the world, or did he just feel like he had to? Would he much rather be a farmer? Maybe. Would he much rather be hanging out with his dad and his mom and his dog? Probably.

Gerard Way

People always accuse me of being motivational in a way, like it was a bad thing, but that's just how I was raised. My mom raised me in a positive environment, with lots of love in my heart, and that reflects in my music.

Lenny Kravitz

I didn't plan on being a single mom, but you have to deal with the cards you are dealt the best way you can.

Tichina Arnold

My mom and dad passed away from cancer. Within nine months, I lost both of my folks. Immediately after that, I had a horrible betrayal where my brother, who worked for me, stole a lot of my money. He's in jail now.

Dane Cook

My mom is definitely my rock.

Alicia Keys

I was always at peace because of the way my mom treated me.

Martina Hingis

I think the most fun part about working on 'Good Luck Charlie' is spending time with everyone, honestly, because everybody on set is like my brother and sister and mom and dad. They're so fun to be around, so that's probably the best part about working there.

Bradley Steven Perry

I want my daughter to be proud of me and look up to me. I think early on in my pregnancy I realized that to be the mom I want to be, I had to change my life, and that's what I'm doing.

Holly Madison

For me, already being part of a single parent household and knowing it was just me and my mom, you'd would wake up times and hope that the next day you'd be able to be alongside your mother because she was out trying to make sure that I was taken care of. But all I cared about was her being home.

LeBron James

I always knew I wanted to have children. When I met my husband, Rande, I thought, 'This is the guy.' When you are getting ready to become a mom, being in love with someone just isn't enough. You need to think about whether he would be a good parent and raise your children with similar beliefs.

Cindy Crawford

It was my 16th birthday - my mom and dad gave me my Goya classical guitar that day. I sat down, wrote this song, and I just knew that that was the only thing I could ever really do - write songs and sing them to people.

Stevie Nicks

I feel like a good mom. I'm a strong woman now... Don't look down on me. Pray for me because I'm trying.

Fantasia Barrino

I think there's a time to work, and everyone has to kind of adjust. And then there's a time to relax, and be the mom or take the kids on vacation when you need to wind down. So it's a matter of planning, and being able to map out your year or your week or let's start with the day. It is just being multi-tasking and being available.

Vanessa Williams

No mother wants to hear her son say he's gay. Those two words rip the picture of a daughter-in-law and grandchildren into pieces. I felt sorry for my mom and wanted her to know everything was going to be all right. But then she said, 'I don't really care, Johnny, as long as I know that you are going to be happy.'

Johnny Weir

When I was 19 years old, both of my parents died in the same year; my mom of cancer and my dad in a car accident. Through the next two or three years and a series of bad decisions - all my own, I might add - I ended up literally homeless, before that was even a word. I even slept occasionally under a pier on the Gulf Coast.

Andy Andrews

For some students, school is the only place where they get a hot meal and a warm hug. Teachers are sometimes the only ones who tell our children they can go from an Indian reservation to the Ivy League, from the home of a struggling single mom to the White House.

Denise Juneau

The best part of being a mom to me is the unconditional love. I have never felt a love as pure, a love that's as rewarding.

Monica Denise Brown

This is the place where anybody - like an African American kid raised by a single mom - can be president.

Jennifer Granholm

Studies show that children best flourish when one mom and one dad are there to raise them.

John Boehner

I love all my fam. I have quite possibly the best dad, mom, and sister in the world.

Ryan Eggold

I've realized how precious life is. When I was younger, I was more adventurous. I felt invincible. I was game for everything. As a mom, I don't want to get injured because then I can't take care of my kids.

Kristi Yamaguchi

You can be good at technology and like fashion and art. You can be good at technology and be a jock. You can be good at technology and be a mom. You can do it your way, on your terms.

Marissa Mayer

If you think back to the first sporting event you went to, you don't remember the score, you don't remember a home run, you don't remember a dunk. You remember who you were with. Were you with your mom, your dad, your brother, on a date?

Mark Cuban

I grew up in a family of Republicans. And when I was 18 and registering to vote, my mom's only instruction was 'You just go in and pull the big Republican lever.' That's my welcome to adulthood. She's like, 'No, don't even read it. Just pull the Republican lever.

Tina Fey

I was born in Corpus Christi, Texas, the youngest of four girls, including my oldest sister, Lisa, who has special needs. My mom was a special education teacher, and my dad worked on the Army base. We weren't wealthy, but we were determined to succeed.

Eva Longoria

There are a lot of people who helped make Queen Latifah who she is today. I don't forget, but a lot of people do and get big heads. My mom will make me walk the dogs or take out the trash when I go home. I'm not allowed to get a big head; I've still got to do the simple things in life.

Queen Latifah

My mom passed away at 41 from diabetes. And I'm 42, thank you. I didn't want to do that to my son. So any time I was at the gym, that thing that helped me do that last squat was my son calling some other woman mommy. And that would just give me that extra oomph to do that last squat. I want to be around for him.

Sherri Shepherd

I remember once in junior high school, on a Friday, my mom came home from work and said to my brother and I,

'You know, between us, we have only 27 cents, but we have food in the refrigerator, we have our little garden out back, and we're happy, so we are rich.'

John Paul DeJoria

I love my mom. My mom loves me. We don't have an easy relationship. I don't think we ever will, but I'd rather have a complicated, misunderstood relationship than have no relationship at all.

Tori Spelling

You may earn whatever money you earn as a cricketer, but you want to play for your country. At the end of the day, you want to do something special. There are plenty of people who earn 50 crores or 100 crores as businessmen or big professionals or who are really doing well in business. But what gives pleasure to your mom and dad is the fame.

Mahendra Singh Dhoni

One thing my mom used to tell me was to look to the other side, and know that my present is not going to be everything. So if I'm having a bad day, she goes, 'Just imagine tomorrow. This is going to be over. This is going to be done with.'

Tyra Banks

My mom passed on her obsession of all things antique or vintage. I love to go thrift store shopping or explore any sort of garage sale. Treasure hunting is a family passion.

Zoey Deutch

My mom and dad gave their kids the greatest gift of all - the gift of unconditional love. They cared deeply about who we would be, and much less about what we would do.

Mitt Romney

My mom has made it possible for me to be who I am. Our family is everything. Her greatest skill was encouraging me to find my own person and own independence.

Charlize Theron

I don't know where my romanticism comes from. My mom and dad would read to me a lot. 'Treasure Island,' 'Robinson Crusoe,' tales of chivalry and knights, things like that. Those are the stories I loved growing up.

Daniel Radcliffe

I look at my father. He is one of my heroes. He is such an

incredible, classy man. He was such a great father and such a great husband in so many ways, and we lived through some pretty tough times losing my mom. When I see all that he did, I think, 'Wow, that's a really wonderful man.'

Emmanuelle Chriqui

When I was about 6, my cousin was very active in a Filipino repertory company, doing musicals and plays. Her aunt was one of the founders of the company, and she told my mom that there were these auditions for 'The King and I,' and that they needed kids. I auditioned, got in and the love affair started from there and just kept going.

Lea Salonga

I love babies, and I have my nephews that I love. I have a great mom and she has raised three kids, so if I take lessons from her, I think I'll be great. All my friends have little brothers or sisters.

Jamie Lynn Spears

I forgive my mom for being a psycho and my dad for being a loser.

Nikki Sixx

I grew up with just my mom. She and I were like best friends. She's a very independent woman and I admire that about her. In my life, I've tried to be like that. To be okay with being on my own and being independent.

Emma Roberts

My wrestling and family go together. It's always been that way, from day one with my mom and dad, my sister, my wife, four daughters, grandsons, son-in-laws.

Dan Gable

I never liked apples. In fact, when I was a little girl, my mom wanted to give me apples in my lunch box and I would ask for green peppers. So bizarre... It's funny - I don't have an apple a day, but I can say that I have a few a week.

Lana Parrilla

I think maybe my mom thought that Katharine Hepburn would be a good role model of, like, a strong, smart, independent woman. Maybe she steered me in that direction. You know, because she was really so ahead of her time.

Gillian Jacobs

I don't have a regular happy family like most people. My parents are separated; my dad married someone else and so did my mom. All my siblings are from my parents' other marriages. So yes, it is complicated, and I don't like talking about it or explaining this to everybody. But all this doesn't stop us from being close to each other.

Shahid Kapoor

My dad didn't graduate from high school, ended up being a printing salesman, probably never made more than $8,000 a year. My mom sold real estate and did it part time.

Al Franken

As a mom, you have all these situations you go through, and you're like, 'What is going on? Is this normal? Is this a phase? Or what is this?' and then you feel silly for asking questions because you think, 'I'm a mom - I'm supposed to know these things,' but you don't.

Britney Spears

My parents are both very funny but they're also relatively soft-spoken, normal human beings while I'm just a lunatic. I don't know where this loud, ballsy, hammy ridiculousness came from. I'm just glad I followed my goals and my parents did too. It's not like we even had a plan when I dragged my mom to Los Angeles.

Emma Stone

My mom used to make my costumes when I was little; she sews a lot. One year, I was a bride and I had a big wedding dress and a bouquet. Another year I was a medieval princess with a long teal dress and a veil. It was a little extravagant, but it was cute!

Sasha Pieterse

My mom used to make everything. She had a great garden and composted and made everything from scratch - peanut butter, bread, jelly, everything. I don't know how she did it because all those things take time and love and labour. I only do half the stuff she does - but there's still time.

Julia Roberts

I've always believed fitness is an entry point to help you build that happier, healthier life. When your health is strong, you're capable of taking risks. You'll feel more confident to ask for the promotion. You'll have more energy to be a better mom. You'll feel more deserving of love.

Jillian Michaels

I really want to adopt a child... I want to be called 'Mom.'

It really is the most beautiful word in the English language.

Patti Stanger

My mom had a job, and she also took care of us, and she also took care of Dad - I always saw her pulling triple duty, doing more than I ever felt like she needed to. I made a promise to myself that it would be more of a team effort in my family someday. And because of that, I became more independent.

Carrie Underwood

Having a child makes you realize the importance of life - narcissism goes out the window. Heaven on earth is looking at my little boy. The minute he was born, I knew if I never did anything other than being a mom, I'd be fine.

Jenny McCarthy

My mom has always wished me a daughter just like me.

Pink

Come Christmas Eve, we usually go to my mom and dad's. Everybody brings one gift and then we play that game when we all steal it from each other. Some are really cool, others are useful and some are a bit out there.

Amy Grant

My parents and my grandfather on my mom's side would travel the earth. They went to Australia and China, and they went to probably every soccer game I ever played.

Brandi Chastain

Hillary Clinton famously talked about how raising a child takes a village. Except our society isn't set up that way. We're organized in nuclear units, and a single mom can ask her friends only so many times for help picking up the kids.

Katharine Weymouth

I am very proud of my mom and consider her the most courageous woman I know. With perseverance, sacrifice and hard work, she raised a family of Olympic athletes and gave us the tools and the spirit to succeed. That is something that my brothers and I will always be thankful for.

Diana Lopez

Sending a handwritten letter is becoming such an anomaly. It's disappearing. My mom is the only one who still writes me letters. And there's something visceral about opening a letter - I see her on the page. I see her in her handwriting.

Steve Carell

Growing up with three older brothers and being the youngest and the only girl, my mom always made me tough. She's taught me over the years how to be a strong, independent woman, how to carry yourself in a positive way and anything that my brothers can do, I can do.

Diana Lopez

My real dream is to have a whole, like, buy a whole piece of land. Imagine, like, a long driveway. Like, a cul de sac-type street, with maybe, like, seven houses. Me be right here. Have my mom be able to be right here. My brother over here. My girl's grandmother and family right here. Friends over there. That's my real dream.

J. Cole

My dad is still Christian Scientist. My mom's not, and I'm not. But I believe in God, and that there's a higher power and an intelligence that's bigger than us and that we can rely on. It's not just us, thinking we are the ones in control of everything. That idea gives me support.

Ellen DeGeneres

My mom used to say that I became a fighter and a scrapper and a tough guy to protect who I am at my core.

Vin Diesel

I love those hockey moms. You know what they say the difference between a hockey mom and a pit bull is? Lipstick.

Sarah Palin

I've never lived my life in the opinion of others. I believe I'm a good person. I believe I'm a good mom. But that's for my kids to decide, not for the world.

Angelina Jolie

I was raised in the greatest of homes... just a really great dad, and I miss him so much... he was a good man, a real simple man... Very faithful, always loved my mom, always provided for the kids, and just a lot of fun.

Max Lucado

The person who has inspired me my whole life is my Mom, because she taught me commitment. She sacrificed.

Mike Krzyzewski

My mom calls me an older soul because, growing up, she taught me stuff real early. Now I spend most of my time chasing wisdom, chasing understanding.

Ray Lewis

A guy is a lump like a doughnut. So, first you gotta get rid of all the stuff his mom did to him. And then you gotta get rid of all that macho crap that they pick up from beer commercials. And then there's my personal favorite, the male ego.

Roseanne Barr

My mom had me at 16 and took me every place she went. I remember going on peace marches. She tried to take me to Woodstock - it was pouring rain. It was on my birthday, and I was crying so much in the car they turned the car around and dumped me at my grandmother's house... I had a little attitude.

Debi Mazar

I grew up in Marcy Projects in Brooklyn, and my mom and pop had an extensive record collection, so Michael Jackson and Stevie Wonder and all of those sounds and souls of Motown filled the house.

Jay-Z

If I could get any animal it would be a dolphin. I want one so bad. Me and my mom went swimming with dolphins and I was like, 'How do we get one of those?' and she was like, 'You can't get a dolphin. What are you gonna do, like, put it in your pool?'

Miley Cyrus

I am a single mom and I'm the breadwinner and I have to work and I have to do these things and that's just the way it is. I don't think my son even knows any different.

Charisma Carpenter

Once you're a mom, always a mom. It's like riding a bike, you never forget.

Taraji P. Henson

It's about getting the kids up and fed, getting one to school, getting the other down for a nap, going to the grocery store, picking one up from school, getting the other one down for another nap, cooking dinner... I live my life at these two extremes. I'm either a full-time stay-at-home mom or a full-time actress.

Jennifer Garner

When I'm not the Tiger Mom, I'm a professor at Yale Law School, and if one thing is clear to me from years of teaching, it's that there are many ways to produce fabulous kids. I have amazing students; some of them have strict parents, others have lenient parents, and many come from family situations that defy easy description.

Amy Chua

I am excited to rise today to support National Mom and Pop Business Owners Day. This celebration honors the husband and wife business owner teams whose work helps drive the economy and fuel job growth.

Melissa Bean

I believe this with all my heart: The greatest coach of all time in my eyes is my mom. She's instilled in me a toughness and a perseverance and just a never-quit mentality, and I thank her every day for providing me, for what she sacrificed her life for.

Scott Brooks

My sisters and my mom, those people help me get through every single day.

Demi Lovato

When love is gone, there's always justice. And when justice is gone, there's always force. And when force is gone, there's always Mom. Hi, Mom!

Laurie Anderson

I know a lot of people who really aren't beautiful because their attitudes are very nasty... Whether I make the 50 most beautiful list or not, I'm always going to feel like I'm number one most beautiful to myself... I get that from my mom, and my daddy and my friends who raised me.

Queen Latifah

I'm a religious person. I remember my mom told me: 'Vengeance belongs to God. It's up to him to wreak vengeance.' It's hard for me to get to that point, but that's the work of God.

Rodney King

I look up to my mom. She's a beautiful woman.

Leighton Meester

My mother wouldn't allow me to speak slang when I was growing up. But when I got outside, around my friends, it was 'Yo' and 'That's the joint' and 'Yo, what's up?' So I had my game for my friends and my game for my mom.

Queen Latifah

Even in high school, I'd tell my mom I was sick of swimming and wanted to try to play golf. She wasn't too happy. She'd say, 'Think about this.' And I'd always end up getting back in the pool.

Michael Phelps

I was brought up by a single mom in a poor town in Arkansas and while some aspects of small-town life were really positive - like the fact that everyone there is really sweet and hospitable - there is also this close-minded mentality, and that naturally made me want to rebel.

Beth Ditto

I remember one time when all the nuns in my Catholic grade school got around in a semicircle, me and Mom in the middle, and they said, 'Mrs. Farley, the children at school are laughing at Christopher, not with him.' I thought, 'Who cares? As long as they're laughing.'

Chris Farley

I was a single mom that raised two bright, beautiful, and compassionate girls.

Connie Stevens

Food feeds both the body and soul - there are clear reasons to eat a balanced diet, but there are also reasons you cling to your mom's secret chicken noodle soup recipe when you're sick.

Michael Mina

My mom was always keen I stayed in school and got good grades, and she was always keen for me to do medicine. I used to go to drama classes when I was younger, and she would always take me. But when I got to an age when I decided it was what I wanted to do, when she accepted it, she had actually been the most supportive person ever.

Iain De Caestecker

I grew up very differently than a lot of other people in my hometown in Mississippi. But I can't imagine my life any other way. I flew home and surprised my best friend at his graduation, and I remember turning to my mom and saying, 'My graduation was so much cooler than this.' I had Melissa Joan Hart give my commencement speech.

Taylor Spreitler

My mom is always telling me it takes a long time to get to the top, but a short time to get to the bottom.

Miley Cyrus

What makes me happy is just curling up in with my mom in her bed and watching a marathon of 'CSI' and 'Grey's Anatomy' episodes with pints of ice cream.

Taylor Swift

My mom and I have always been there for each other. We had some tough times, but she was always there for me.

LeBron James

It wasn't so long ago that I was a working mom myself. And I know that sometimes, much as we all hate to admit it, it's just easier to park the kids in front of the TV for a few hours, so we can pay the bills or do the laundry or just have some peace and quiet for a change.

Michelle Obama

It's usually my mom who gets on me about my facial hair.

I can't grow a good mustache, so I guess it's just a neck beard. I just have trouble growing up there.

Andrew Luck

I told my mom, 'I'm not buying another magazine until I can get past this thought of looking like the girl on the cover'. She said, "Miley, you are the girl on the cover,' and I was, like, 'I know, but I don't feel like that girl every day.' You can't always feel perfect.

Miley Cyrus

God blessed me with two unbelievable parents, and I am just like both of them. I have the smile and charisma of my mother and the big heart of my mom, because she wants to save the world and help the world, so I am just like her.

Magic Johnson

From the moment this baby came into our home, those two dogs have never been more in love. It's the most beautiful thing I've ever witnessed. People keep saying, 'Oh, you're a single mom.' I'm like, 'Actually, I'm not. I've got two boys helping.'

Charlize Theron

For me, just being how old I am, I know I don't want to be a single mom. I really would rather make it a two-person job. But I've also come to terms with not being a mother at all. I'm actually really good with either direction that my life can take as being a valid experience.

Lisa Edelstein

My mom is going to kill me for talking about sleeping with people. But I don't want to put myself in the position where I'm in a monogamous relationship right now. I'm not dating just one person. 'Sex and the City' changed everything for me because those girls would sleep with so many people.

Lindsay Lohan

My mom told me as a youngster I was always intellectual, like as far as being able to adapt fast and quick. But I had a fun childhood, went to regular school.

Chris Brown

These days it's cool to be ethnic and to be different, but when I was a kid, it was not cool - at all. My friends would come over and my mom would make crepes with eggs, stuffed with mozzarella cheese, tomatoes and spinach. And they'd be like, 'What is this?'

Giada De Laurentiis

I was thinking that when I have children, that I should always dress as a character for them, so they think their mom is Alice in Wonderland or Cinderella. It would be totally messed up!

Gwen Stefani

I was brought up as an only child, and we were very close. But when I was 14, we got evicted. We came home to a padlock, and I looked up at my mom and she was crying, and there was nothing to do.

Dwayne Johnson

My mom has always said that if I get a big head, she'll take me out of this business as quickly as I got into it.

Chloe Grace Moretz

I'm sure there were times when I wish I had thought, 'Gosh, that might really embarrass mom and dad,' but our parents didn't raise us to think about them. They're very selfless and they wanted us to have as normal of a college life as possible. So really, we didn't think of any repercussions.

Jenna Bush

My mom says I'm a fighter, a fierce competitor, and I think I am, too.

Gabby Douglas

For many women, going back to work a few months after having a baby is overwhelming and unmanageable. As strange as it may seem, things get even more difficult for a working mom after the second and third baby arrive. By that time, the romance of being a modern 'superwoman' wears off and reality sets in.

Mika Brzezinski

As a small business owner for the last 15 years, when I think of what truly changed my life, it was my faith, a strong family, my mom did a really, really good job of encouraging me in very clear and discernible ways.

Tim Scott

I always think about which blood drive was going on in Georgia that day when that husband or mom or school teacher rolled up their sleeve and actually gave me a second chance at life. It's the ultimate gift of life, and I'm the one who was on the other end.

Niki Taylor

At 3 years old, I was imitating and doing fun little commercials for the family. Then at 5, I knew, 'OK, this is something I really like.' At 8, I was crying in front of the mirror and my mom was like, 'Oh boy, here we go. We know what she's going to do.'

Lana Parrilla

Dad needs to show an incredible amount of respect and humor and friendship toward his mate so the kids understand their parents are sexy, they're fun, they do things together, they're best friends. Kids learn by example. If I respect Mom, they're going to respect Mom.

Tim Allen

My mom was a single mother, raising my sister and me. My mom has an incredible talent for living in the world without traditional structure, and her friend, who was in advertising, put me in a commercial when I was five. It was just to make money.

Gaby Hoffmann

Being a Hot Mom means being respected as a mom and a woman. And, the key to being a Hot Mom is having a sense of humor about yourself and all the crazy situations that arise.

Jami Gertz

People think I have courage. The courage in my family are my wife Pam, my three daughters, here, Nicole, Jamie, LeeAnn, my mom, who's right here too.

Jim Valvano

I just love food, especially my mom's Bulgarian cooking. Taco Bell is my favorite fast food restaurant. I also love Italian food.

Leah LaBelle

One day I went up to my mom and I said, 'Mom, can I have permission to build a 2.3-million electron-volt atom smasher - a betatron - in the garage?' And my mom stared at me, and she said, 'Sure. Why not? And don't forget to take out the garbage.'

Michio Kaku

Sometimes when you are a great mom, you're not so great at your job. And then when you're good at your job, you're not so great of a mom or a good wife. It's a dance that never stops. But it's beautiful.

Gisele Bundchen

My mom, Irmelin, taught me the value of life. Her own life was saved by my grandmother during World War II.

Leonardo DiCaprio

I remember watching the Grammys and looking at the performances and crying to my mom, saying how much I wanted to be there.

Christina Aguilera

Mom and Pop were just a couple of kids when they got married. He was eighteen, she was sixteen and I was three.

Billie Holiday

Mom spent the time that she was supposed to be a kid actully raising children, her younger brother and younger sister. She was tough as nails and did not suffer fools at all. And the truth was she could not afford to. She spoke the truth, bluntly, directly, and without much varnish. I am her son.

Chris Christie

My coaches were great. My mom and dad. My dad never missed a wrestling meet.

Dan Gable

When I was in nursery school, the teachers asked me, y'know, 'What does your dad do for a living?' So I said 'He helps women get pregnant!' They called my mom and they were like, 'What exactly does your husband do?'

Natalie Portman

Call it the Tiger Mom effect: In the business world today, failure is apparently not an option.

Naveen Jain

I've always wanted to be a mom because I want to give a kid all of the magical gifts my mom gave to me, such as love and friendship. She and I had this incredible connection that was so unbelievable.

Jennifer Love Hewitt

My mom was sarcastic about men. She would tell me Adam was the rough draft and Eve was the final product.

She was a feminist minister, an earth mom who wore a bra only on Sundays.

Daphne Zuniga

My humanitarian work evolved from being with my family. My mom, my dad, they really set a great example for giving back. My mom was a nurse, my dad was a school teacher. But my mom did a lot of things for geriatrics and elderly people. She would do home visits for free.

Cat Cora

My mom put me and my sisters in the water to feel comfortable, to have water safety.

Michael Phelps

My mom enlisted in the U.S. Navy in World War II, and my parents actually bought our home thanks to the loan she got through the GI Bill.

Thomas Friedman

Postpartum depression is a very real and very serious problem for many mothers. It can happen to a first time mom or a veteran mother. It can occur a few days... or a few months after childbirth.

Richard J. Codey

My mom put me away at 7. I enjoyed it... Being in institutions, I got three meals a day, clothes.

DMX

Being a mom makes me feel whole and like I understand the meaning of life.

Rebecca Romijn

If you go from a structure where you have the support and that partner and that construction of a family and that's broken apart, I think that's probably a lot harder than always being a single mom and having the father being a support in another area.

Bridget Moynahan

When I was younger, my sister thought it was funny to pretend to punch me in the face because my mom was concerned about my teeth falling out. They were loose for a long time, and she knocked out my teeth.

Amy Adams

It was rough being dark. I got heat from my own people more than anyone else. I remember going to my mom and saying, 'Why am I so black?' And she said, 'Because I'm black. You just gotta always work harder than the average bear.'

Bernie Mac

In Hollywood, you play a mom and instantly, you've got osteoporosis.

Gabrielle Union

I like to work. The self-esteem and satisfaction that I get from working makes me a better person, which makes me a better mom.

Cindy Crawford

My mom did not have money. She was a single mom, on and off in periods between marriages. My husband, however, grew up on a wonderful farm in Tuscany, in Florence, and his family was so entertaining in terms of growing their own food and using the fruit of their land. We have very, very different experiences.

Debi Mazar

I always say I am a realist, and my mom says, 'No, you just have anxiety.'

Jessica Chastain

I learned from my mom to always keep pushing yourself.

Gabby Douglas

You don't realize how hard it is to live on your own. But there's no mom to do your laundry, and make you dinner and to do things for you, and you don't think about little things like buying paper towels and salt.

Emma Roberts

My pops and my mom started playing Marvin Gaye and the Isley Brothers and all these people, but at the same time, they always had Snoop on right behind it in the same mix.

Kendrick Lamar

My mom often tells me to get married, but she gets it now that I don't want to. Like any other mom, she is worried, but she also understands the demands of my profession. I am blessed to have a family like this.

Randeep Hooda

My daily schedule is quite hectic, but I have to put my health first in order to be the best mom and wife I can be.

Ellen Pompeo

I have to admit I was dismayed when I found out 'type A' refers to a category of risk for heart disease - I thought it was just a nickname my mom gave me!

Reese Witherspoon

As an actress, I have put myself out there as an independent black woman, a single mom, a go-getter, a hustler who isn't afraid to survive.

LisaRaye McCoy-Misick

For me, the spirit of Christmas means being happy and giving freely. It's a tradition for all the kids in the family to help mom decorate the tree. Christmas is all about family, eating, drinking and making merry.

Malaika Arora Khan

I hope telling the story of how I went from being a single mom to serving in the Texas State Senate to running for governor will remind others that with the right leadership in government, where you start has nothing to do with how far you go.

Wendy Davis

When I was 26 or 27, I gave up journalism. I came to England after my mom died, to let serendipity take its course. And I just found myself back in journalism again.

Heather Brooke

I'd rather be dealt with as a person than a persona. With my children, I'm just 'Mom.' At the end of the day, the position is just a position, a title is just a title, and those things come and go. It's really your essence and your values that are important.

Queen Rania of Jordan

I like bad boys, and I like to take them home to my mom.

Priyanka Chopra

My mom used to tell me that the most valuable thing she owned was her library card. We were poor, but that's not what she was talking about. My mom knew that education opened doors and opened minds.

Richard Carmona

My mom's the one I look up to for everything. I feel like I'm a lump of clay and she's moulding me into a woman.

Chloe Grace Moretz

When I was a child, I wanted to be an actor, but I had really bad buckteeth. I didn't want to get braces, but my mom said I couldn't be an actor if I didn't get the braces. So, I got the braces.

James Franco

My brother Jim and I spent many wonderful summers working on dairy farms in Wisconsin owned by Mom's cousins, and as members of our local Boy Scout troop.

Peter Agre

I was always pushed to do that much more, and in the long run that made me more of an MMA fighter. My mom always told me that if I let it go to the judges, I'd lost. There was no way I was going to win a decision, so I had to find ways to finish the fight fast.

Ronda Rousey

I'm an immigrant kid who came to America from India when I was very young and grew up in New York City with a single mom and really was influenced by all of those immigrant cultures bumping up against each other.

Padma Lakshmi

There was a point - when I was a kid - where I said I wanted to be like Luke Skywalker, with blond hair and blue eyes. My mom right there told me to never be ashamed of who I am.

Chaske Spencer

I started modeling when I was - not older, but not 12. I have a mom who's a feminist - she's an English professor, an intellectual. She really gave me the equipment to understand that you can celebrate yourself without putting yourself down or needing to apologize for the way you look. I think that attitude is really crucial for a model.

Emily Ratajkowski

Sometimes when my mom finds a fun article and really wants me to read it, I will. But I prefer to just kind of focus on what I want to do and not really what other people are saying, because I don't want that to affect me too much.

Missy Franklin

One thing I hear a lot is, 'Dude, my mom loves your record,' or 'I got it for my dad for Christmas.' I'm essentially doing dad rock. Which is great, because I love Steely Dan, you know? Nothing wrong with dad rock!

Mac DeMarco

Coming up in the Bay Area and being African American in a city that has a history of complex issues of violent crime, interaction with the police is always intense. That's something you have to learn. My mom taught me at a young age that if ever a cop stops you, you put your hands up and freeze - don't move.

Ryan Coogler

Most people, almost everyone knows of a teen mom. Teen pregnancy rates are growing, and we need to bring awareness to that.

Madisen Beaty

Whenever something went wrong when I was young - if I had a pimple or if my hair broke - my mom would say,

'Sister mine, I'm going to make you some soup.' And I really thought the soup would make my pimple go away or my hair stronger.

Maya Angelou

I'd go to, like, six different schools in one year. We were on welfare, and my mom never ever worked.

Eminem

My mom was on the United Way group that decides how to allocate the money and looks at all the different charities and makes the very hard decisions about where that pool of funds is going to go.

Bill Gates

I wanted to be in 'Star Wars' when I was six years old. I asked my mom for two years, and she told me I was crazy.

Jennette McCurdy

My mom always makes the whole family pile into the car and drive around to look at the Christmas lights. My brother and I never want to do it, but my mom just loves it!

Debby Ryan

My mom has obviously had a powerful influence on my life, and her voice can describe certain things that I couldn't see in myself.

Common

My mom and I have always been really close. She's always been the friend that was always there. There were times when, in middle school and junior high, I didn't have a lot of friends. But my mom was always my friend. Always.

Taylor Swift

For everything I do, I think about a 6-year-old girl and her mom that I saw at my concert last night. I think about what those two individuals would think if I were at a club last night. I never want to be arrested, and I never want to get a DUI, those are my moral values.

Taylor Swift

As a mom I know that raising children is the hardest job there is.

Hilary Rosen

I've been my mom's kitchen helper since I was a little kid.

Taylor Swift

I became an actress because my mom wanted me to become an actress. It took me until my mid-30s to realize I actually didn't. I actually wanted to write and direct and be more involved in politics and humanitarian issues.

Angelina Jolie

When my mom ran for the Senate, my dad was there for her every step of the way. I can still hear her saying in her beautiful voice, 'Why should women have any less say than men, about the great decisions facing our nation?'

Mitt Romney

When you are getting ready to become a mom, being in love with someone just isn't enough. You need to think about whether he would be a good parent and raise your children with similar beliefs.

Cindy Crawford

When I turned about 14, I developed a friendship with this guy whose mom was the secretary to Ernest Angley, the faith healer, who's very popular in the Midwest. He had a television show, and he was sort of like Liberace mixed with Jerry Falwell - very glitzy, very high-tech.

Marilyn Manson

I'm a lioness. I have four cubs. I'm a mom. I want to take care of my kids and protect them.

Heidi Klum

My mom said the only reason men are alive is for lawn care and vehicle maintenance.

Tim Allen

I honestly don't even know how I got into acting. It happened so quickly because my mom and sister used to do commercials, and apparently when I was little I would unbuckle myself from the stroller and crash their auditions.

Bailee Madison

Something my mom and I have always said to each other is: 'We're not here for interviews. We're not here to get your picture taken. We're here to make a difference, and this is our opportunity to.'

Bailee Madison

My mom never taught me to be waiting for some prince on a white horse to swipe me off my feet.

Tyra Banks

I hear my friends and my mom tell me I'm special, but honestly, I still don't get it.

LeBron James

My mom was such a strong character. I don't want to say she was like a man, but she was tough.

Lance Armstrong

We come from fallible parents who were kids once, who decided to have kids and who had to learn how to be parents. Faults are made and damage is done, whether it's conscious or not. Everyone's got their own 'stuff,' their own issues, and their own anger at Mom and Dad. That is what family is. Family is almost naturally dysfunctional.

Chris Pine

Being the only man in the household with my mom definitely helped me grow up fast.

LeBron James

When I was 5, some financial things happened, and I moved seven times in a year. We moved from apartment to apartment, sometimes living with friends. My mom would always say, 'Don't get comfortable, because we may not be here long.'

LeBron James

My mom, she wasn't like a baseball mother who knew everything about the game. She just wanted me to be happy with what I was doing.

David Ortiz

My mom and I are very close.

Lady Gaga

I grew up in a makeup chair. And to see the women around me getting ready was so aspirational. It's about mothers and daughters, a girl watching her mom at a vanity table.

Drew Barrymore

As far as I'm concerned, there's no job more important on

the planet than being a mom.

Mark Wahlberg

Thankfully, I have my mom and a small group of close friends who are there for me 24/7 and whom I can trust and depend on.

Christina Aguilera

I grabbed my mom and I went to the couch and I said, 'Mom I want to ask Jesus to come into my heart.' And I got on my knee and I asked Jesus to come into my heart, forgive me of my sins, and make me a child of God.

Tim Tebow

My mom and I have always been very close. She is my best friend. She had to make a lot of sacrifices early on in my life to make sure I got to do what I wanted to do.

Norah Jones

Being a mom has made me so tired. And so happy.

Tina Fey

My mom and I had the same vision, and we want the same things. We would always make a goal list every year.

Kim Kardashian

My mother was a Sunday school teacher. So I am a byproduct of prayer. My mom just kept on praying for her son.

Steve Harvey

I went to see 'Phantom of the Opera' with my grandma and my mom when I was very little. The stage, the voice, the music... Composer Andrew Lloyd Webber has been a massive inspiration to me for some time - the storytelling, that deliciously somber undertone in his music.

Lady Gaga

I made some truly awful movies. 'Stop! Or My Mom Will Shoot' was the worst. If you ever want someone to confess to murder just make him or her sit through that film. They will confess to anything after 15 minutes.

Sylvester Stallone

My mom decorated with lots of antiques. I never liked it when I was a little girl - I wanted to live in a modern house. But now I love it.

Paris Hilton

I never had, like, a nanny that took care of me. My mom always fed me breakfast, lunch, and dinner.

Miley Cyrus

No press, no television. If my mom calls and says, 'Did you hear about?' I don't want to know nothing about anything that is going on in relation to music. I shut it all off.

Lady Gaga

Looking back, I think I was always musical. My dad was very musical, and I think my mom was musical.

Paul McCartney

As a mom, you worry about protecting your kid. But there are extra added layers of fears when you're talking about a kid with autism or who has some special needs issue.

Holly Robinson Peete

My mom took all of my behavior personally. Everything I did, she thought it was an act of rebellion against her. But it was just me being me.

Pink

I'm simply the mom who makes the lunch, drives to school, finds where the toys are, washes the clothes, and I'm here to play. And that's all I should be.

Sandra Bullock

I probably have an earlier curfew than anyone. My mom wants to keep me really safe and my dad's not overly protective, but he's a dad no matter what.

Miley Cyrus

My problem is that my imagination won't turn off. I wake up so excited I can't eat breakfast. I've never run out of energy. It's not like OPEC oil; I don't worry about a premium going on my energy. It's just always been there. I got it from my mom.

Steven Spielberg

My mom is at my house every day, and she nags me about everything, especially hygiene.

Shia LaBeouf

My parents were working class folks. My dad was a bartender for most of his life, my mom was a maid and a cashier and a stock clerk at WalMart. We were not people of financial means in terms of significant financial means. I always told them, 'I didn't always have what I wanted. I always had what I needed.' My parents always provided that.

Marco Rubio

I promised my mom that if, after a year of putting 150 percent into my career it didn't work out, I would go back to school. I never did go back.

Queen Latifah

I love being a single mom. But it's definitely different when you're dating.

Brooke Burns

Mom was 50 when my Dad died. She got on a bus every weekday for years, and rode 40 miles each morning to Madison. She earned a new degree and learned new skills to start her small business. It wasn't just a new livelihood. It was a new life.

Paul Ryan

My dad was a bartender. My mom was a cashier, a maid and a stock clerk at K-Mart. They never made it big. They were never rich. And yet they were successful. Because just a few decades removed from hopelessness, they made possible for us all the things that had been impossible for them.

Marco Rubio

I make a lot of mistakes, too, and I'm constantly re-evaluating how I'm doing things and trying to be better every day, whether it's as a mom or taking care of myself.

Mia Hamm

Never play cards with a man called Doc. Never eat at a place called Mom's. Never sleep with a woman whose troubles are worse than your own.

Nelson Algren

Being a mom, it feels like I did something so powerful and amazing. It's such a gigantic blessing, and a confirmation that the Creator exists. And all of that has made me feel sexier and stronger. I call it 'lava in my spine.'

Jill Scott

My Mom said she learned how to swim when someone took her out in the lake and threw her off the boat. I said, 'Mom, they weren't trying to teach you how to swim.'

Paula Poundstone

The best situation is being a single parent. The best part about is that you get time off, too, because the kids are with their mom, so it's the best of both worlds. There's a lot to be said for it.

Larry David

My inspiration was my mom. She's a great cook, and she still cooks, and we still banter back and forth about cooking. Growing up in a mostly Portuguese community, food was important and the family table was extremely important. At a very young age I understood that.

Emeril Lagasse

My dad believes in God, I think. I'm not sure if my mom does. I don't.

Daniel Radcliffe

I think the real heroic teachers are the ones who work with kids, like my mom and my sister do.

David Duchovny

I remember driving to North Carolina when I was a little girl in a snowstorm to get down to my mom's family in the Carolinas. There were chains on the car - it was the late sixties - and we were just singing in the car. Christmas carols.

Tori Amos

I didn't come from a trailer park. I grew up middle class and my dad had money and my mom made my lunch. I got a car when I was sixteen. I'm proud of that.

Kid Rock

There was always music in our home. My mom and my dad loved music. I remember when we were kids we would have these great parties at the house with congas and bongos and African drums, and it was amazing. It wasn't until years later that I found out that they were actually Black Panther meetings.

Queen Latifah

My mom was always really healthy and cautious about her diet, so I'm not a big sugar guy.

Paul Walker

I think in a lot of ways unconditional love is a myth. My mom's the only reason I know it's a real thing.

Conor Oberst

After my mom died, there was so much written about her fashion and her style and all that, and I felt that one of the most important parts of her was missing, her real intellectual curiosity.

Caroline Kennedy

My nursery school did a production of 'The Three Little Pigs.' I played the third pig. When the wolf knocked on my door, I refused to get up and answer it because, to me, he was knocking the wrong way. I just lay there, snoring away on stage, fully immersed in my character. My dad turned to my mom and said: 'Dustin Hoffman.'

Zooey Deschanel

I used to work at a school as a teacher's assistant, and my mom is a principal at an elementary school. I don't know, I think that's a pretty good life, teaching kids.

Conor Oberst

I didn't understand that I could sing until I was like 11 or 12. My mom heard me singing around the house and she said, What are you doing? You really can sing! So then I started going to school and singing to the girls.

Chris Brown

My mom has always been my champion. She was very smart and grounded. She said, 'Save your money. Pay your taxes. Don't put everything in one basket,' but she let me explore and be creative.

Queen Latifah

When I moved out of my mom's house at 18 I was almost as sad to leave her sewing machine behind as anything else.

Beth Ditto

Mom is the most unconditionally loving person I will ever know, and she has always supported me on every level.

Rashida Jones

I was given baby doll toys myself, and they proved a stark reminder that my life was expected to revolve around childbearing - just as my mom's had before me, and her mom's had before her.

Beth Ditto

Being a singer is all about me. About ego. Being a mom is all about being selfless - two different worlds.

Gwen Stefani

I don't want to have kids for like 10 years. I still have a lot to do. I don't even know if I could handle a dog right now. I'm so not ready. Someday I'll be a mom but not until I'm in my 30s.

Avril Lavigne

Because sorry to say, women run the house. They run the family. They hold things up. I mean, it's like you don't ever see your mom get sick because she handles everything. And it's kind of amazing I think to show people just how strong women are.

Sophia Bush

My whole life has been nothing but trying to find a way to take care of my mom and take care of my family as quickly as possible.

Derrick Rose

I'm a soccer mom. I'm T-ball, soccer, karate, homework, keeping them on their schedules. I love being the snack mom, when I get to bring the cut oranges. I have one of those coolers with wheels. I'm at every game, every practice, sitting on my blanket. I love it.

Pamela Anderson

I think I would make a lousy stay-at-home mom. It just wouldn't suit me.

Claire Danes

When you're a mom to three children, nothing bothers you. Trust me. Who cares what people say? I've got other things to deal with.

Faith Hill

My mom took me to see Carnal Knowledge and The Wild

Bunch and all these kind of movies when I was a kid.

Quentin Tarantino

The biggest empty space, the biggest gap in what should be a premier and always vibrant food scene in America is that we don't have hawker centers like they do in Singapore, basically food courts where mom and pop specialists can set up shop in fairly hygienic little stalls all up to health code making one dish they've been doing forever and ever.

Anthony Bourdain

I'm not a figurehead for anything. I was a single mom with two kids. What else was I going to do? It was either be in a band or be a waitress.

Chrissie Hynde

One of the greatest, smartest things I ever did was give my kids Angie as their mom. She is such a great mom. Oh, man, I'm so happy to have her.

Brad Pitt

My father wasn't really involved and my mom is the light in my life.

Marion Jones

I was always a drama queen. I remember playing in the kitchen, trying to get my mom to think I was dead and call the police. When she didn't, I would cry. I was always theatrical. I don't think any of my relatives are surprised.

Amy Lee

Mom and Dad would stay in bed on Sunday morning, but the kids would have to go to church.

Lynn Johnston

I'm lucky that my real-life Mom has both a great sense of humor about herself and an amazing ability to slip into complete denial if the subject matter gets a little too close to home.

Cathy Guisewite

My mom would take me to restaurants, and the first thing I'd ask for would be a pen and a napkin, and I'd sketch shoes and shoes and shoes.

Alexander Wang

To be honest, I wish I had more mom friends.

Britney Spears

I do work too hard sometimes, but my mom is such an inspiration. She tells me to 'chill out' and not take things so seriously. She will say: 'Go and have a massage.'

Josh Peck

I went camping one time when I was twelve, to the Great Lakes. My friend stepped in really deep muddy water and started screaming and sinking. My mom ran up, and I was just standing there a foot away and wouldn't stick out my hand to pull him up. So I'm probably not the best person to take on a camping trip.

Norman Reedus

I'm not blaming my mom for my life because I am responsible for me, and nobody can change me or ruin me easier than I can.

Mindy McCready

Dad was the pitching coach, while Mom was the emotional supporter. Her unconditional love was great, and she wanted what was best for me.

Jennie Finch

My brother's a grip. My mom's a scriptwriter. My dad's a director. So it's like, at heart, I'm a below-the-line girl.

Kristen Stewart

My family, you know, are all still, you know, very close. We're all still very close. Mom and Daddy are still alive. So, what more can you ask for? Your kids are healthy.

Reba McEntire

My mom and dad got divorced when I was very young, and growing up in a family where the head of the household wasn't a man made a big difference.

Dave Mustaine

My mom's whole side of the family, they're all Packers fans. My mom's a Bears fan. My stepdad is a Vikings guy. So that gets ugly. My mom sits upstairs watching the Bears game; he sits in the basement. They can't watch it together. Football's a violent anger in our family dynamic.

Ashton Kutcher

We all seek approval, and our mother's seal is usually the most important. The nitty gritty is that we have to accept ourselves, even if it is just to be ready for the next cut-down. Mom's blessing or not.

Beth Ditto

My mom was always saying: 'Be whatever you want to be, but stick with it. Don't waver. Don't change who you are for anybody.'

Miranda Lambert

My mom has always been my support system. She taught me to never give up and to keep pursuing my passions no matter what.

Mandy Moore

You do need parental guidance and I was in a great position with both my mum and dad. They split when I was a baby but even though I stayed with my mom they were both very much involved in my upbringing.

Leonardo DiCaprio

TV family sitcoms have always been about fathers who know best and mothers who are so enchanted with everything they do. I wanted to be the first mom to be a mom on TV. I wanted to sent out a message about how us women really feel.

Roseanne Barr

The real estate agent had to go door-to-door in the apartment building we wanted to rent, asking if it was OK for this interracial family - my mom is white and I was a 1-year-old half-African kid - to live in the apartment building.

Tom Morello

My mom is very confident and she was always a role model of mine.

Ashley Tisdale

We never had a bathtub. Mom would bathe me in the wooden or tin washtub in the kitchen, or in a big lard can.

Ethel Waters

More and more couples are having this negotiation or discussion, but I'm still amazed at the number who aren't and where the cultural norm sort of kicks in and they just assume that mom's got to be the one who stays home, not dad.

James Levine

My mom's always been a good cook, so I took a lot of stuff from her, but most of the stuff I took from Emeril or Bobby Flay right off the TV and make it. I just loved to cook, so it just became a thing. It's a release. Even if I'm alone, I'll cook a full meal, maybe even a two-course meal, just because I love to cook. It's my secret love!

Christian Kane

Boxing is individual, although there's a team concept because you need a great corner, you need a great trainer, you need a great prep man, you need all of these things, but it's more of a Mano a Mano; it's more you versus me. I miss that time in training camp and Dad and Mom cooking meals. It was one big family.

Sugar Ray Leonard

When you're sick, nobody takes care of you like your mom.

Trisha Yearwood

I think it's a tough road if you're a stay-at-home mom, a

working mom, if you have a partner, if you don't. It's the best job in the world, and the toughest job in the world all at the same time.

Angela Kinsey

My mom drives me crazy sometimes, but I have a good relationship with her.

Seth Rogen

The family on my mom's side, their whole business is inventing and pitching stuff. My grandfather is in infomercials. He's a pitchman, so if you're ever watching TV late at night, you'll probably see him pitching knives. My great-grandfather also invented the plastic cheese grater.

Ashley Tisdale

My dad never blew anything up, but he probably had friends who did. He and my mom have always preached that the pen is mightier than a Molotov cocktail.

Joseph Gordon-Levitt

I was born and raised in the high desert of Nevada in a tiny town called Searchlight. My dad was a hard rock miner.

My mom took in wash. I grew up around people of strong values - even if they rarely talked about them.

Harry Reid

I'm a mom - I'm lucky if I get to shower in the morning. Luckily, nail polish stays on my toes. I've been so bad on the upkeep, though.

Idina Menzel

I'm more straightforward, and I speak up more than I did before. When I was younger, I wouldn't speak up as much, but now that I'm a mom, things have changed.

Britney Spears

Every day, my mom and I would watch a different Judy Garland VHS. I love how she tells a story when she sings. It was just about her voice and the words she was singing - no strings attached or silly hair or costumes, just a woman singing her heart out. I feel like that doesn't happen that much anymore.

Ariana Grande

My mom, she is the most unbelievable mom that you could ever have in your entire life and she's always with me on everything. The most I've ever been away from her is two days. I love her more than anybody could ever know.

Dakota Fanning

There's nothing more frustrating than when fans use a nickname. That's like people you don't know using names from people that you're intimate with. Like if my mom has a nickname and a fan finds it out and starts using it, that's creepy.

Evangeline Lilly

I'm not sure anyone - and I could be wrong in this - grows up thinking, I want to be a single mom.

Bridget Moynahan

All of us kids ended up 'doing Mom.' There are four of us who've tried show business. Five if you insist on counting my sister the nun, who does liturgical dance.

Bill Murray

I'm very close with my family, so my mom is part of my entourage.

Kid Cudi

That's actually how my parents met. They were pen pals. My mom was in the Philippines and my father was in the States, and they wrote to each other. He went out to meet her, and they wed not too long after.

Vanessa Hudgens

The hardest thing for me is planning ahead. My mom was brilliant at it.

Faith Hill

My mother was a single mom, and most of the women I know are strong.

Regina King

Mom never quit on me. My only regret is that she didn't live long enough to share some of the money and comforts my work in show business has brought me.

Ethel Waters

My mom never wanted to be a grandmom. She never wanted to be a mom, really.

Pink

Now, if you're Al Gore, you can afford $10 a pop for squiggly-pig-tailed fluorescent light bulbs. But if you're mainstream America, two or three kids, mom and dad working outside the home, that's not a very good deal.

Joe Barton

What does good in bed mean to me? When I'm sick and I stay home from school propped up with lots of pillows watching TV and my mom brings me soup - that's good in bed.

Brooke Shields

Once in high school, I completely over plucked my left eyebrow all the way up to where you're not supposed to. I had no idea what I was doing and it looked terrible! My mom was like 'What did you do to yourself?' I was so embarrassed.

Ashley Tisdale

I want to make my music and be a happy woman, a good wife, a good mom and one day hopefully have a child of my own.

LeAnn Rimes

I'm raised by a single mom and didn't have pops around for the most part of my life. And she, by any means necessary, gave me the best opportunities that she knew how to give me.

Shemar Moore

I used to say, 'Man, I think I'd be a really good dad. I'll be a great provider. I'm funny; I'll go on trips with them - I'll do all sorts of stuff.' But the momming? I'm not made for that. I have a really good mom; I know what she put into it.

Elizabeth Gilbert

Privacy is relational. It depends on the audience. You don't want your employer to know you're job hunting. You don't spill all about your love life to your mom or your kids. You don't tell trade secrets to your rivals.

Barton Gellman

My hat was pulled down and this girl said 'Are you really him?' I whispered 'Yeah, I'm really him.' She screamed, 'Mom! Dad! It's Heath Ledger!

Josh Hartnett

Being able to take care of myself is something that my mom really instilled in me.

Stevie Nicks

I got my first tattoo when I was 16 years old and I went with my mom to get it done - she has a bunch too so we're tattoo buddies now.

Josh Hutcherson

Dad was the pitching coach, while Mom was the emotional supporter. Her unconditional love was great, and she wanted what was best for me. It was more about what she did than what she said, and she made sure I was the best I could be.

Jennie Finch

I did find some time to go to a record store and check out 'Headstrong' actually in the racks. It was pretty cool; I never thought I'd see my own CD sitting there with everyone else's. I made my Mom take lots of pics!

Ashley Tisdale

No matter how good you are, at some point your kids are gonna have to create their own independence and think that Mom and Dad aren't cool, just to establish themselves. That's what adolescence is about. They're gonna go through that no matter what.

Eddie Vedder

On Halloween, don't you know back when you were little, your mom tells you don't eat any candy until she checks it? I used to be so tempted to eat my candy on the way to other people's houses. That used to be such a tease.

Derrick Rose

Growing up, my mom was very strict about how I dressed and how I behaved, and I said to myself that I wasn't going to be like that. But now I know I'm going to be exactly like my mom. I'm going to be worse!

Nicole Scherzinger

Oftentimes, even as a little kid, I would get up before anyone else. My brother would still be sleeping, my mom would still be sleeping, so I would literally play 'Monopoly' by myself. I would play board games; I would do things by myself.

Will Ferrell

My mom taught me how to sew when I was 2 or 3, so I've been sewing for as long as I can remember.

Serena Williams

I wanted Cathy and Irving to actually say 'I do' and be pronounced husband and wife on Feb. 5, which is my mom's birthday.

Cathy Guisewite

Every kid needs to say, 'I want what my mom and dad have.'

Josh McDowell

Dad was in the British Army and my mom was in the Royal Air Force, so both of my parents believed in discipline.

Mike Myers

Mom always tells me to celebrate everyone's uniqueness. I like the way that sounds.

Hilary Duff

My mom always encouraged me, it was never weird. She'd look at 'Heavy Metal' and go 'Woo-hoo!'

Zack Snyder

My mom was an amazing singer and music was a big part of my life, so I grew up listening to Nat King Cole, Johnny Mathis, Henry Mancini; I used to watch 'The Andy Williams Show' on TV. I was very musical, so I was watching stuff that most kids my age wouldn't be interested in.

Gloria Estefan

Most children - I know I did when I was a kid - fantasize another set of parents. Or fantasize no parents. They don't tell their real parents about that - you don't want to tell Mom and Dad. Kids lead a very private life. And I was a typical child, I think. I was a liar.

Maurice Sendak

Food brings back memories. I had a mom that wasn't a good cook, so I would eat my grandma's food. It was amazing because it brings back a time almost in Technicolor. I see her house, I see her stove; I think about what it felt like when I was sick, and it felt like love.

Debi Mazar

I could never have pictured myself writing a book when I was 25 years old. My mom was an English teacher but I wasn't that way growing up.

Tony Dungy

There were definitely bands and musicians I liked that drove my mother insane. I probably liked them all the more for it! Bjork drove my mom nuts. What I listened to was actually pretty mom-friendly for the most part. I wasn't very rebellious.

Gillian Jacobs

The most important thing in my father's life? World peace. Me and my brother. My mom.

Sean Lennon

I've never had siblings, I didn't grow up in a big family; it was just me and my single mom. And hectic family dysfunction was actually something that I craved.

Emmy Rossum

Fact: The new '90210' is cooler than the old '90210.' It's the lithe, streamlined Skipper to the elder series' venerable Barbie. Gone are the traditional parents - they've been replaced by a hipster mom n' pop who get busted necking in the car.

Diablo Cody

Although I have a lot of close female friends in my life, my number one is still my mom. Without her, I wouldn't have the values that I have and see the world the way that I do today. She taught me how to appreciate and respect women. She taught me chivalry and how to love a woman and respect their feelings and emotions.

Shemar Moore

Everything I am is because of my mom.

Sarah Michelle Gellar

My mom was always the supplier of soccer balls, and so people were always knocking on my door, and trying to get me out so we could play.

Freddy Adu

My mom raised me to be clean, so it's in my nature. I have two little girls, and I'm married, but we've got a nanny and a maid.

Vanilla Ice

My mom died when I was 16. I had a rough childhood, you know what I mean, but it made me strong.

Travis Barker

My mom passed away a day before high school started, and her dream was for me to be a full rock and roll guy, and play drums in a band.

Travis Barker

Mom was a smoker. My grandfather was a smoker. My aunts were smokers. My uncles were smokers. I don't know any smokers now, not even my mom.

Jane Smiley

I'm a proud strict mom and, you know, I'm really proud of the two daughters I've raised. And I'm especially proud of my relationship with them. We're very close. I think we're good friends.

Amy Chua

I remember that my mom, my dad and I would play different roles in mock debates, where one of us would be the moderator, one of us would be my dad - frequently not my dad - and then one of us would play his opponent.

Chelsea Clinton

My first paying job might have been doing a play, actually. My mom paid me to dress up as a flounder at my sister's 'Little Mermaid' - themed birthday party when I was little.

Paul Dano

The health benefits of paid sick days policies are obvious. They prevent the spread of disease. But the impact is wider. If a working mom or dad loses a job because of sickness, the family may slip into poverty.

Madeleine M. Kunin

I just got my phone back yesterday. My mom had it for two days. I was supposed to read a book and I really wanted to play Call Of Duty.

Chloe Grace Moretz

When you're adopted, no matter what, you've got issues with unconditional love. And you find out you're the product of the worst situation for a young girl to be in and start her life, and I'm so grateful that my birth mom made the decision she made. She came from a rough situation.

Rodney Atkins

I've always wanted to be a mom. I had a great relationship with mine. I'm ready to pass on to my child all the great love that my mom had for me.

Jennifer Love Hewitt

My family, they're story tellers. My mom is Irish, and my dad is Italian. In my family, we weren't allowed to watch TV while we ate - we had to sit around the table and tell stories about our day.

Meg Cabot

My mom raised me to never have anything control me.

Chris Tucker

I always figured there would be a kid audience and an adult audience, and there is. That's true for 'Hunger Games' and 'Twilight' and 'Harry Potter.' And 'Maximum Ride,' for sure. In particular what happens is a lot of parents share the books with their kids, and the mom has read it, and the kids, and they talk about it.

James Patterson

Growing up my whole life, my mom was telling me how incredible and special I was and that I was going to change the world. I think it's important for girls to know that they can change the world, that they do have an impact.

Ashley Greene

My mom just wants to make sure that my heart is always in whatever I do and I'm in things for the right reasons.

Kevin Durant

Like a lot of you, I grew up in a family on the ragged edges of the middle class. My daddy sold carpeting and ended up as a maintenance man. After he had a heart attack, my mom worked the phones at Sears so we could hang on to our house.

Elizabeth Warren

It was tough being a single mom. It was tough being in a divorce with children. Very, very hard.

Melissa Etheridge

When I was in the 9th grade, on Halloween night, when you're supposed to go and out and burn your city, my mom made me go to 'Cirque du Soleil.' I was kicking and screaming. This girl came out onstage, and I was instantly mesmerized. I dropped out of school and became obsessed with her. I saw the show, like, 70 times.

Troy Garity

My mom was a single mom, and she had enough on her plate. I knew when I was doing something I wasn't supposed to, and I tried to keep her from finding out about it. I did a pretty good job of that.

Jason Aldean

I live in, literally, the same home when I was swiping my first bank card and wondering if I'd have to put back the Charmin. We still don't have a dishwasher. My mom has done all these gardens so now my house looks like the garden shack in the middle of Versailles.

Rachael Ray

President Obama's fight for rural America is personal. He was raised by a single mom and grandparents from Kansas. He hails from a farming state, Illinois.

Tom Vilsack

I am blessed to have Mom and Dad.

Kevin Eubanks

My parents are wonderful, and I'm really lucky - but my mom has always been almost exclusively a right-brained person.

Brandon Boyd

Also, my mom and family are very important to me and I know that this is not expected.

Christina Milian

We busted a lot of family secrets with this. But to make a long story short, my parents relationship was built heavily on security issues for my Mom, and when my Dad couldn't provide security, the relationship unraveled.

Kenny Loggins

I remember failing my Princeton interview. My mom wanted me to apply because ever since I was a kid she had this dream that I would apply to Princeton, but it was just not happening.

Tina Fey

My life has always been with my dad. Since I can
remember, I was raised by my father my entire life. So he's
kind of been that mom and father figure - always.

Apolo Ohno

A friend of my mom's was a casting director so, really as
kind of a lark, I had a couple of acting jobs that had just
enough exposure to give me the option to continue if I
wanted to. I followed through with it.

Ben Affleck

My mom can't defend herself to the world. She is such an
amazing woman, with such an open heart. It's a real hard
line, and I crossed it. I took everyone's life story and
assumed it would be a great thing to put on screen. I was
being selfish and I feel so horrible about it. I feel so guilty.

Nikki Reed

I am compelled to continuously see the bright side. It is in
my DNA. My kids look at me and say: 'Mom, you're so
happy!' And I do feel happy. I feel joyful inside. I can't

explain it.

Goldie Hawn

My dad had always been a big decaf coffee drinker. But my mom had always been more of a tea drinker. So I grew up around a lot of tea. And I also really love tea. But I'm not one of those people who has ever felt the need to choose between coffee and tea. I think that is a completely false dichotomy.

Chelsea Clinton

My mom FedExes a red velvet cake she makes from scratch to me every birthday.

Molly Sims

I shoplifted. I was about five years old, and I took a candy from a store. We paid for three of them, but I took four, and I went home and cried. My mom took me back, and I paid for the missing piece.

Carrie-Anne Moss

My very sassy, older southern sister is very quick to point out that it's a luxury that my daughter gets to come to work with me. She does, and I have lunch with her every single day. My mom says I have 'high class problems.'

Angela Kinsey

I don't spend a lot of time online. My mother's really good at picking out if she sees a really great review, and she'll forward it to me. She's like my little Internet filter. It's always nice to see something going up; if I want to find something on Nathan Fillion, I do know where to look, but I've got a nice little delivery system in my mom.

Nathan Fillion

My mom used to tell me when I was little, 'When it rains, it's God's manifestation - a big day's waiting to happen.'

Gabby Douglas

Anything that opens you up emotionally is going to impact your acting. Parenthood, becoming a mom, certainly does that.

Keri Russell

One of my most sentimental items is my grandmother's engagement ring that my mom gave me a few years ago. It's a Victorian-style setting that's closed in the back, so it doesn't sparkle the way diamonds do now. I wear it as a pendant.

Georgina Chapman

Not to be weird, but I still have an ongoing relationship with my mom, even though she passed away, and I've been surprised at how much I've been able to convey to her. Now I sound like a total weirdo, but that's true.

Mindy Kaling

My father left... but I tell my mom - and I told my mom this when I was a kid - I said, 'You know what, Mom? Good thing he left because you're a strong woman.'

J. R. Martinez

I was raised in Boston by three older brothers and a very strong and empowering single mom.

Eliza Dushku

Our parents are obviously proud, but they're still trying to get used to the fact that we're in a band. I have a feeling my mom would actually like One Direction if I wasn't in it!

Zayn Malik

The biggest change for me as a mom was realizing I needed to put someone else before me. Now the hardest part about the empty nest is learning to put myself first.

Kim Alexis

Every day I'd come home after school, pop the hood of my mom's car, put alligator clips on the battery, and wire into the house and go play on my computer. If I used it for too long, I'd wear down the car battery, and my mom would be all mad at me the next day.

Ryan Holmes

My mom was a folk singer and Celtic harpist. My dad was in a barbershop quartet and my great grandma was an opera singer. As I grew up, I discovered pop music and Top 40 radio, but it was in the '90s, so music was very different then - it was really lyrical.

Skylar Grey

It's always been my mom and I against the world.

Brittany Murphy

I learned a lot from my Mom. My favorite lesson: remember there is no such thing as a certain way to parent and to remember that you are learning along with your child - it's ok to make mistakes.

Regina King

I played with dolls until I was 15. My mother encouraged it because my older sister got married when she was 15, so Mom thought that the longer I stayed with dolls, the better.

Linda Evans

I can't help but recall my dad and mom. Depression era kids, 8th and 9th grade educations, clawed and scratched to make a living as dairy farmers their whole life. At least two drought cycles nearly took it all away. They just worked harder, longer... and they made it.

Bob Beauprez

My mother was a working woman, and I was alone a lot. So I wanted to be a stay-at-home mom.

Donna Karan

When I turned 18, my mom, my nana and I all went and had tattoos of our favorite Bible verses put on the inside of our wrists. Mine is 1st Timothy, 4:12.

Jordin Sparks

But to sustain a marriage for 50 years, you have to get real a little bit and find someone who is understanding and who you can grow with. My mom always says, 'Marry the man who loves you a millimeter more.'

Ali Larter

I'd say that if you had a strained relationship with your mom, for whatever reason, the best thing to do is be open with each other, talk it over, try and work it out somehow as opposed to just putting a wall up and pushing them away.

Victoria Justice

It's tough growing up where I grew up. My family is very small and really tight. Just being around the neighborhood, my brothers were always around. I didn't want to be in any trouble because I knew my mom or brothers would find out. I didn't want to hurt their feelings. I just tried to do everything right.

Derrick Rose

Every day in our house is like Valentine's Day. I've kept it traditional with what my dad has done with my mom. Every morning, I get up and I make coffee and I bring Giuliana coffee in bed.

Bill Rancic

I think a good mom is an awake mom. At least for me, I've always been a kinder, better person awake than sleep-deprived!

Lisa Loeb

I knew that I was a gay boy fairly early; what was interesting to me was that my mother didn't know. She made me play baseball - I had no desire to do that. I said, 'Mom, I don't like direct sunlight, I don't like bugs, I don't like grass, and I'd rather be in the house playing with your fabric samples.'

Nate Berkus

My earliest memories of my mom were of her multi-tasking - preparing dinner while checking on homework and housework; clearing the dinner plates while setting out bowls for breakfast; making sure we ate our breakfast while lining up bread, lunch meats, apples, and snacks assembly-line style so we could make our lunches.

Christine Pelosi

I was blessed, because I come from a family where they knock you down before you float away. I have a lot of brothers who just make sure we have our feet on the ground, and my mom is a rock star. She is an amazing mother.

Kellan Lutz

If I made a list of the people I admire, Mom would probably fill up half of it. She could do anything and everything.

Patsy Cline

I just think that there's so much judgment in the world, whether it's coming from women in general or from men onto women - it's a lot. And when it comes to being a mom, I wish everyone could band together and realize that everyone has different beliefs, different styles, and different things that work for them and their family.

Hilary Duff

Whether or not we communicate it, I definitely seek my mom's acceptance and approval for everything. She has a strong commercial sense of movies and is a quintessential audience. When she doesn't like something, I know there is reason to worry. When she loves something, there is reason to celebrate.

Karan Johar

I remember, my mom didn't have any help, so if she needed to be somewhere after school, we'd just go down to the neighbors' and she'd give us a snack and make sure we did our homework. There weren't any latchkey kids.

Jennifer Garner

I guess if you are making more money than your mom and dad, you can set your own boundaries.

Alexa Vega

My real name is Amethyst. It sounds like a stage name. My mom is kind of crazy.

Iggy Azalea

I grew up with the Highwaymen, which was Johnny Cash, Willie Nelson, Waylon Jennings and Kris Kristofferson. Mom and Dad rode rodeo, so country music was always in the house and the car. They threw in some Dolly Parton, too.

Christian Kane

Deep down, my mom had long suspected I was gay...
Much of her anger and hurt came from her sense of
betrayal that she was the last to be told.

Chaz Bono

I know that might sound silly coming from someone my
age, but I remember on my 14th birthday having a crisis
like my mom should be having. I kept thinking that I was
getting older, and I haven't really accomplished anything. I
remember thinking that I better accomplish something real
soon.

Q'orianka Kilcher

I've looked at pictures that my mom has of me, from when
I was four years old at the turntable. I'm there, reaching up
to play the records. I feel like I was bred to do what I do.
I've been into music, and listening to music and critiquing
it, my whole life.

Dr. Dre

My dad was Jewish. My mom is not. So I was not raised
anything.

Matt Lauer

It was probably in third grade - I had a super-fake gold herringbone chain. Yeah man, it was, like, super fake. I don't remember if it was my mom's or how I got it, but ever since then, I've loved chains. The first real chain I got was from Kanye. It was a Jacob the Jeweler Kanye West Jesus piece.

Big Sean

I love getting my nails done. My mom's best friend is a manicurist. When I was little, she'd do little paintings on my nails, like flowers.

Miranda Cosgrove

My mom is just someone who's easy to talk to and hang with. My sister, it's always cool to be able to help her out with things. My brother is fun when we're just joking and messing around. And my dad is someone who's helpful with my music and easy to talk to about that stuff because he understands me in that sense.

David Archuleta

My mom and dad met at UCLA when he as a captain in the Air Force and she was in her junior year.

Tracy Austin

Miami Beach - that's where I grew up, in a middle-class Jewish family led by my maternal grandfather. Me, my great-grandmother - a Holocaust survivor, who was my roommate - my grandparents, my mom and her brother all shared a four-bedroom house.

Brett Ratner

Like every mom, you try to juggle, but I also want people to know that you don't have to be a superhero. I'm not a superhero; I have a team of people who help me. I have a great family support system.

Kimora Lee Simmons

My mom gives me an allowance. She keeps me pretty tight-reined.

Chloe Grace Moretz

My mom was at every single game I played as a kid, rain or shine.

Ryne Sandberg

It's like I've experienced quite a weird and unusual life, you know, being with a mom who's a single parent and struggling with money and things like that. It's really hard. And it brings a lot of other insecurities in life and a lot of other issues in life, in school and a bunch of other things.

Fefe Dobson

My mom is real passionate and a family-first woman. She always told me that just because I can shoot a basketball better than someone else, I shouldn't think that I'm better than them. I know if I change, my friends and family would lay me down. She just wants to see her kids do right.

Derrick Rose

Puffy's contribution to hip-hop culture was the remix. He offered us the music that his mom played in front of him, with newer drums and younger artists. That worked, and will consistently be there. The remix comes right after the original record, that's something Puffy did to influence the culture.

Curtis Jackson

Sunscreen is my number 1, 2, 3, 4, and 5 tip. I'm a fanatic, partially because I live in L.A. and have fair skin and freckles, and partially because of my kids. My mom always made me wear sunscreen and I'm trying to be that mom for them.

Alison Sweeney

Dilip Kumar was the only Bollywood hero who could make a girl shiver just by looking at her. If you don't believe it, ask your mom!

Imtiaz Ali

Well, when I was a little girl we had 17 cats once. They all lived outside, and they kept having more kittens. My mom made us put little ribbons around each kitten's neck, put them in a wagon, and go door-to-door around the neighborhood to try to give them away.

Cheryl Hines

Mom was a housewife; Dad was an accountant. They taught me a lot about the value of working hard.

Irene Rosenfeld

On my mom's side I'm Mexican, and my dad is a white dude.

Tyler Posey

I have the biggest sweet tooth! You name it, I will eat it. My all-time favorite is my mother's butter cake. Every time I go home, my mom will already have the cake made because I love it so much. This makes my siblings mad because they think she favors me. I don't care because she probably does!

Michael Strahan

When I was younger, on weekends, my mom would make us pancakes with our initials on them and then a tiny cup of coffee. I remember at 10 sneaking my own coffee and pouring a ton of sugar in and going up to the playroom and drinking it.

Mary-Kate Olsen

I want somebody like my mom. My mom is a very charitable woman. She's the sweetest woman in the world. I'm looking for the second sweetest woman in the world. I'm looking for honesty and a big heart.

Jason Derulo

The thing was, at a young age, my mom and my grandma always tried to keep me out of the streets as much as they could, so they put me in a private school when I was super young.

Big Sean

My mom was a huge Adam and the Ants fan. My granddad listened to a lot of Motown and Elvis and Johnny Cash. So I was kind of well-rounded.

Hayley Williams

My mom always does this thing where, the closer I get to home, the more she calls. 'Hey, listen, how's your plane? Did you land? Are you landing? Sweetie. Listen. We want to... ' The anxiety amps up exponentially as I get closer, and then I can't get out fast enough.

Maria Bamford

My mom cooked pot roast with noodles and frozen vegetables. Or she'd make spaghetti or hot dogs, or heat up TV dinners. Before I started modeling at age 19, I was 5'8" and weighed 165 pounds.

Carol Alt

I grew up with a pretty tough mom. She was a self-appointed neighborhood watchdog, and if she saw that any of the local boys were up to no good, she would scold them on the spot. Although she is only 5 feet 2, she was famous in our neighborhood for intimidating men three times her size and getting them to do the right thing.

Hanna Rosin

Minimalism? It is something I appreciate as an art form but leave to others - unless you count a collection of warhorse-workwear Yves Saint Laurent trouser suits. Maybe my penchant for hippie-deluxe eccentricity came from an escapist dream of a different world. It was tough being a working mom in the 1970s.

Suzy Menkes

Being a mom is what life is about. I hope people realize what the priorities in life should be and know not everything has to be perfect.

Kourtney Kardashian

I have used Twitter for so many things, from places to stay, places to go, things to do, things I need, medical advice, you name it. Especially when I'm on tour, it really feels like I'm being taken care of by half a million people. It is like having a mom.

Amanda Palmer

I want a partner in crime and a Bonnie to my Clyde. I've just been so focused on my career. Women don't like being number two, so I've been glad to keep my distance so I could focus on me, get my life together and take care of my mom without disappointing the woman I love.

Shemar Moore

As a kid, I did some running but especially loved biking and swimming. I grew up on Long Island, and our mom took us all the time to the ocean, so I grew up doing open-water swimming in the Atlantic.

Alice Dreger

My mom and dad worked very hard to give me the best chance in - not just in golf but in life. You know, I was an only child, you know, my dad worked three jobs at one stage. My mom worked night shifts in a factory.

Rory McIlroy

My mom won't let anyone treat me like a little princess.

Chloe Grace Moretz

The one thing my mom will let me get is a nice shoe sometimes.

Chloe Grace Moretz

The problem with me is, anything that's easy I will just overdo it. Especially with clothes. But I'm 14 - my mom is super-strict about that.

Chloe Grace Moretz

My mom was in a punk rock band called The Trash Women, and they toured and all of that. She had me when she was 17.

Kreayshawn

I'm a really bad liar. My mom finds out every time, especially now that she's got Facebook.

Pixie Lott

I was a hyper kid in school and the teacher suggested to my mom she needed to do something with me.

Devon Sawa

Mom and sister played piano growing up; my grandma still plays piano in church. They always beat me over the head trying to get me to play piano, but I was more interested in riding dirt bikes and playing in the mud.

Dustin Lynch

Both my parents were amateur badminton players. My father is a scientist and wanted me to be a doctor. But my mom was very aggressive and loved badminton. She pushed me right from the age of nine to take up the sport.

Saina Nehwal

Being a working mom is not easy. You have to be willing to screw up at every level.

Jami Gertz

My mom was the first African-American woman to graduate from the University of Chicago Law School, in 1946. She had leadership roles in the law, in government and the corporate world. She was a great role model in that she felt anything was possible.

John W. Rogers, Jr.

I never let anyone pluck, including myself, unless my mom approves. She guards my eyebrows. She's like the eyebrow police!

Isabelle Fuhrman

You know the things I went through as a youngster, coming into the business, all the good, the bad and the ugly that came. I'd had a rough life. I grew up single parent. My mom, she was like a father to me.

Raekwon

Red certainly is the family color. From my mother and my grandmother, I've learned a lot of little tricks - the significance of color and lipstick being one of them. I started skating when I was eight years old, and my mom did my makeup for me back then.

Gracie Gold

My mom was the picture of the blue-collar mom: Two and three and four jobs to make sure that me and my sister never needed, that was her thing.

Ne-Yo

As a busy working mom I'm always pressed for time, so a quick and easy beauty routine is key!

Angela Kinsey

I had ridiculous amounts of energy. Mom's like, you're driving me crazy - do you want to try gymnastics? From the moment I started it, I loved it and it kind of was like storybook from there.

Alicia Sacramone

Luckily, I was raised by a kind of gypsy family, which is why I always get along better with people who worked in circuses than with kids of other actors. My mom was so carefree with us in a beautiful way. We were used to sleeping anywhere.

Lou Doillon

When I was young, I had two older sisters, and since I was the youngest in my family, my mom took me around with her all the time. I was forever with her when she was having coffee in the middle of the afternoon with her three sisters. And they would talk about men. I absorbed a lot of that.

Richard LaGravenese

Having seen my mom in community volunteer work my whole life and in Congress for 25 years, it is true as she often says that she sees her service as an extension of her role as a mother and a grandmother.

Christine Pelosi

My mom is very structured. She gets up, she does her prayers, and she eats her oatmeal with blueberries and Greek yogurt, and she has her prayer list, and she doesn't worry too much about things.

Maria Bamford

I wanted to perform well for my mom and dad, because in high school, I didn't have a job. My brothers, they worked at Pizza Hut or places like that, but sports, that was my way of giving back.

Junior Seau

My mom and dad put my brother and sister through university and they were very keen for us to have an academic background just to give us a chance.

Rob James-Collier

I have no regrets. I had an amazing surrogate who carried my son for me. I am so grateful to her. I can even say I am grateful for having cancer. I was always meant to be a mom, but if I didn't have cancer, I never would have had

Zev. I would have had a kid, but not Zev, and I want Zev - tantrums and all.

Marissa Jaret Winokur

I probably wouldn't be singing if not for Michael Jackson. When I started singing, I didn't like my tone until my mom put me on to Michael Jackson and Stevie Wonder, so listening to the way they used their instrument helped me get more comfortable with my own.

Ne-Yo

My dad is a very quick-witted, sarcastic, dry, humorous guy, whereas my mom's very silly, and that side of the family is very musical.

Tim Heidecker

My mom didn't believe in putting chemicals in hair. But when I got to college, we didn't have A/C in our dorms freshman year. So after several days of waking up looking like a Chia Pet, I was like 'OK, I'm gonna get a perm.' And then my hair revolted and fell out. I was over that quick, fast and in a hurry.

Keshia Knight Pulliam

My mom didn't write, but she loved to read. She liked books 'that made you a little nervous.' Stephen King, Dean Koontz and Peter Straub were the three wise men of our family bookshelf.

Michael Easton

The film I do doesn't have to be a film that only my kids can watch. My kids will watch films, but I will decide what they watch and not. My aim is to play different characters and not be stuck in a mould. Just because you are a mom and a wife doesn't meant you have to play those roles, even in films.

Madhuri Dixit

I gotta be honest with you. I'm kind of jealous of the way my dad gets to talk to my mom sometimes. Where are all those old-school women you can just take your day out on? When did they stop making those angels?

Bill Burr

I can't say for sure where I was headed the first time my mom put a blue blazer on me. Church, probably. West Side Presbyterian in Ridgewood, New Jersey, specifically, where my blazer was paired with a clip-on tie and a pair of khakis for a Sunday morning with my fellow congregants.

Willie Geist

Like a lot of kids, I had a Superman cake or different theme cakes, but then I hit the age where I think my mom thought I was ready for the German chocolate cake that she makes for my dad. Just the sight of that, the taste of that frosting, just reminds me of being at home with my mom and my dad and my sister and my friends.

Willie Geist

That's a big deal for kids, when they come into the kitchen and the teacher is drinking coffee with mom. They react differently on the next day when you say: 'Sit down and shut-up!'

Ed O'Neill

I have a hard time waking up. No alarm clock works! It sounds childish, but I seriously have my manager, my mom or a buddy of mine wake me up if I have to be somewhere. It's a serious issue! I've been very late for some serious gigs because of it!

Jesse McCartney

I want to thank my mom, Brenda Rose. My heart, the reason I play the way I play, just everything. Just knowing the days I don't feel right, going to practice, having a hard time, I think about her when she had to wake me up, go to work and make sure I was all right. Those were hard days.

Derrick Rose

I wanted to marry a girl just like my mom.

Michael Bergin

I like my name. My mom named me after a song by the 1970s group Bread. So, it's meaningful, and I like the song. It's a love song - kind of - but it's kind of depressing and dark.

Aubrey Plaza

They see me as being this Super Mom on TV who also can more than handle a difficult husband, and they assume I'm going to be just full of wisdom as a mother and wife myself.

Patricia Richardson

I have so many pieces that once belonged to my mom and both of my grandmothers. All of these pieces are very sentimental, and I love to wear them. I also have many pieces from my father that I probably cherish the most. I love wearing his dress shirts.

Kourtney Kardashian

I used to play Donna Karan. I used my dad's home office, and Kim was my assistant. Then one of our friends would play a buyer, and I would take her to my mom's closet and show her the new collection.

Kourtney Kardashian

Childfree women are actually great assets to the planet. Our carbon footprint is smaller than a mom's! And we have enough money to write checks to organizations that help kids get vaccinations, vitamins, and educations yet have plenty of free time to advise your daughter that one day she will regret piercing her lip.

Jen Kirkman

I was always into fashion because my mom has always been interested in fashion. She majored in fashion merchandising in college, and it's always been something we have in common.

Dakota Fanning

When I was growing up, Forest Park was full of integrated

families. It was amazing. One my best friends was Vietnamese. Another one was half-Mexican, half-black. Another one was from Colombia. Another one was born in the U.S., but his mom was from Germany and spoke with a German accent. So we all had multiple identities.

Dinaw Mengestu

My mom is two people to me. She's my mom number one, and then she's this lady most comedians know as being a legendary owner of a nightclub that's responsible for starting a lot of heavy careers.

Pauly Shore

My mom has this great skiing event in Jackson Hole, Wyoming, every year for a local charity.

Joely Fisher

My father came from Germany. My mom came from Venezuela. My father's culturally German, but his father was Japanese. I was raised in New York and spent two years in Rio. My parents met at the University of Southern Mississippi, and they had me there, and then we moved to New York. I'm not very familiar with Mississippi.

Fred Armisen

I'm always just carrying a Tupperware cup, ever since my mom went to a Tupperware party and got 'em. I've left them strewn all over the U.S. and Europe. I drink iced tea out of them.

Si Robertson

We were poor. But my mom never accepted that. She worked hard to become a residential contractor - got her master's with honors at the University of New Orleans. I used to go to every class with her. Her father was my paternal figure.

Frank Ocean

When you come to L.A. as a kid with your mom, you're lured into doing things that you think are cool and fun and a good idea, but they're cheesy and awful. And recording a pop single was one of them.

Penn Badgley

There are some good teachers out there, but the only one who is a genius at diagnosing my swing is my mom. She took up golf late, when she was 39, but in her younger days, she was an amazing athlete. She never read an instruction book or took lessons, but she has a remarkable eye for motion.

Boo Weekley

When I was 12 I cried to my mom, because I never got my letter to Hogwarts.

Sara Paxton

When I first got into the entertainment industry, I would always watch Rihanna and all those people, so I was like, 'Ooh, I have to be this.' So my mom was like, 'Just be yourself.'

Willow Smith

I was actually the one who decided to move to LA. Mom and I were driving on Sunset Boulevard during one of our trips back to see her family, and I said, 'Can we just stay?' So we did.

Lily Collins

I'm Mexican-American. My dad was actually born in Mexico. He was raised up there, and he came back and forth to America pretty much his whole teenage years. My mom is from Sacramento, California, and she's a blonde-haired, blue-eyed girl. She's a whitey.

Ryan Guzman

I had amazing intellectual privilege as a kid. My mom taught me to read when I was two or three. When I was five, I read and wrote well enough to do my nine-year older brother's homework in exchange for chocolate or cigarettes. By the time I was 10, I was reading Orwell, Tolstoy's 'War and Peace,' and the Koran. I was reading comic books, too.

Chris Abani

I credit my mom with inspiring in me a love of design, matched by her creative problem-solving abilities. This is a woman who could find an old, discarded piece of furniture, bring it home and turn it into something fabulous.

Candice Olson

My mom once lost track of me at the zoo and when she found me I was lecturing a man about the difference between dromedary and Bactrian camels. I was about 3 1/2.

Patrick Rothfuss

I was growing up with a single mom who'd be at work when I came home from school. So I'd just turn on the TV. I grew up watching old Clint Eastwood westerns. I adopted him as one of my male role models.

Bailey Chase

My heroes always are mostly my parents - my father especially, and my mom, who's passed on already. My dad is a very strong man, and by him being educated, and a principal and school superintendent over 37 years, he plays such a big role in my life.

Dikembe Mutombo

I believe destiny and hard work go hand in hand. I was studying to be an engineer when my mom and my brother sent my pictures for the Miss India contest. I didn't even know about it. If that isn't destiny, what is?

Priyanka Chopra

I have a rebellious teenage thing. If my mom says I can't do it, I'm gonna do it. But I'm pretty good. That's why it was fun to play Sam in 'The Bling Ring.' I got to be someone crazy and wild to the extreme, then go home and relax and get rid of the burden.

Taissa Farmiga

There's no one else I would rather have as my manager

than my mom because I know that she has our best interests at heart. Sometimes, it's hard to separate manager mode from mom mode. I think as our manager, my mom will get more emotional about situations than she would if she was just our manager.

Kourtney Kardashian

When I was 10 years old my mom used to play Tupac while she cleaned the house.

Soulja Boy

My dad is a bank president and my mom was an accountant and they didn't think that seeking the life of a freelance writer was very practical, you see. Of course, I was just as determined to do it.

Kevin J. Anderson

I was looking to do something non-fiction because I had done a strip, 'My Mom Was a Schizophrenic.' I really enjoyed the process of doing that strip, despite its subject matter. To do it I'd had to do a lot of research and reading and I figured I'd like to do that again.

Chester Brown

Starting in my teens, I was always standing on the corner near our apartment singing harmony with friends. We'd also go to the park and sing under the bridge near the lake for the echo. When it was cold out, we'd stand in the little heated lobby in the project's administration building, where my mom paid the rent each month.

Frankie Valli

I am the first one to go to university in my family. I am the first writer as well. My dad is a retired policeman, and my mom works for a glass-processing company. She is health-and-safety manager, and my stepfather is a plumber. I have four half siblings, one from my mom's marriage and three from my dad's marriage, so we are kind of scattered.

Samantha Shannon

My mom has accepted my style. My dad is a little suspect with all the bright colors and loud stuff. He's a khakis and polo kind of guy. He's OK with it, but the loud stuff, he says I'm his little daughter.

Chandler Parsons

My mom bought me a white Strat, but that wasn't what I wanted, so I went to a guitar store in Cleveland and - the guy told me it was a really good deal - made an even swap for a blue Teisco Del Ray. I loved that guitar and used it a bunch.

Dan Auerbach

From a very young age, music was very much in my house. I would sit with my mom, with the old LPs, listening to The Beatles and Carly Simon and Lionel Richie. The old LPs used to have the lyrics. From there, I would put on dance and music displays for my family, just to entertain them and make people laugh and smile.

Lara Pulver

Growing up I always shopped at Victoria's Secret with my mom and saw Angels like Gisele and Karolina Kurkova in the windows.

Lindsay Ellingson

I think it was my mom's attitude about art and being part of the narcissistic digital generation or whatever that made me think anyone would care what I had to say about anything!

Tavi Gevinson

I think my first big purchase was actually for my mom. She had one of those '90s TVs in her living room that's like a 10x10 brick, so I purchased her a flatscreen for her living room.

Dave Franco

For me, being tall was very positive because I thought my mom was the most beautiful person ever.

Lisa Leslie

My mom has always been a huge inspiration. She was a single mom raising two kids in New York. Now that is full-on all the time.

Kim Raver

I was at a photo shoot, and I was wearing a cross necklace that my mom bought me, and somebody made a joke like, 'Why are you wearing a cross? Like you would be religious.' And then they took it away. I was really affected by that. The whole thing made me realize that I do want a cross with me at all times.

Kate Upton

I always had a standard of, back when I was doing the country music I always told people I would never record a song that I wouldn't sit down and sing in front of my mom and dad.

Ricky Skaggs

I lived in South Africa until I was 11 when we first immigrated. My mom had sent me back there when I was 14 for summer vacation. I wasn't doing very well in school, my grades were slipping. I called my mom one day and told her that I wasn't coming back. I ended up staying there until I was 17 before coming back to North America.

Kandyse McClure

My mom makes something called green pie, which I thought was a delicacy that many people only had at Thanksgiving, but it turns out it was just Jell-O with whipped cream on it. And it's delicious.

Bobby Moynihan

My mother is the most incredible woman on this entire Earth, and she's so giving and loving and sweet and she always raised me how to forgive and forget and move on. She's the catalyst behind it all, my mom is. And I'm 100% a momma's boy!

Brody Jenner

My mother and my grandmother are pioneers of Mexican cuisine in this country, so I grew up in the kitchen. My mom, Zarela Martinez, was by far my biggest influence and inspiration - and toughest critic.

Aaron Sanchez

My mom worked as a pharmacist, but she is one of the best storytellers I know. My sister is a gospel and opera singer and my brother, who passed away, was a writer.

Tunde Adebimpe

I was really lucky. My gal pal was my mom.

Ana Ortiz

As a little kid, not only is my dad Jo-Jo White, but M. L. Carr is involved in the family, Red Auerbach is my godfather, and my stepmother was an Olympic-caliber sprinter. Athletes were all around. I happened to be a natural athlete. If I wasn't, it might have been hell. But I never got any pressure from my mom and dad to be an athlete.

Brian J. White

I have a 16 year-old son, so I'm now a soccer mom. I stand

on the sidelines and I hear the things parents are saying, so I want them to understand what it is their kids are feeling in any sports environment.

Brandi Chastain

I spend a lot of time at my son's school and I really wanted to do a movie that the kids could see. The good thing about being my age and not having to be the ingenue anymore is that I get to be a mom. I get to have kids in my movies.

Virginia Madsen

I know Spanish pretty well. I'm half-Puerto Rican - my mom is from Puerto Rico - so I have a lot of family there, and my mom's first language is Spanish. But growing up in the States, and with my dad being from the States, I'm kind of just like this white kid.

David Lambert

I'm married to a white man, and then my daughter came out looking like the whitest white child with blonde hair and blue eyes. And I'm like, 'Omigosh, now what am I going to do?' She has my mom's features and is lighter than my husband. And my boy is browner than I am. Brown eyes and really tan.

Karyn Parsons

I was discovered in Paris when I was there on a school trip at the age of 13. After that, my mom came in contact with Elite Amsterdam; then I started modeling.

Maud Welzen

I don't think I would have been able to stick with it and been proud of who I am and be feminine out on the court. I think I would have folded to the peer pressure if I didn't have my mom to encourage me to be me and be proud of how tall I am.

Lisa Leslie

I'm named after a horse. My mom's best friend had a horse named Brooke, so my dad suggested 'Brooklyn' as a more formal version, and it just stuck - and now I live in Brooklyn part-time, so go figure.

Brooklyn Decker

I suddenly had this really mad desire to have an affair with a woman. I was divorced. I was childless. I figured there's got to be one more way to really tick off my mom.

Carol Leifer

Since I've become a mom, I'm more about comfort and simplicity. I'm essentially a jeans girl, and I dress them up or down with accessories.

Jessalyn Gilsig

My mom was a professional fitness competitor, so I go into the gym with her. I train with my dad and mother. It's embarrassing, because she's really strong.

Booboo Stewart

My earliest memory is seeing Michael Jackson in Melbourne with my sister when I was about ten. I still have this souvenir stick with a glove that would light up and make a peace sign in a bunch of different colors. I'm so happy my mom didn't throw that out.

Emilie de Ravin

I'm a huge breast cancer awareness advocate because my mom went through breast cancer recently. It really brought our family closer.

Brenda Song

My favorite subject was English, and I wanted to study English abroad when I was young, when I was a kid, but my mom said 'No, it's too dangerous to go abroad by yourself.' So I gave up.

Doona Bae

Just recently I was in Target with my mom shopping, and out of the blue, I see this father and his two daughters and he says, 'Can they get a picture with you?' And I'm thinking to myself, 'Am I the one millionth customer or something?'

Atticus Shaffer

My mom taught me to go after my dreams. I have this faith in myself that I must have gotten from her.

Amy Jo Johnson

I know this is kind of corny, but we thought about renewing our vows again because I think my mom would really love it if we did that in Arkansas, where I came from.

Mary Steenburgen

I was more of the kind of babysitter that liked holding the baby, sort of playing Mom, and then putting the baby to bed and watching TV while eating everything in their kitchen.

Ari Graynor

Cancer has been unfortunately in my life. My mom's best friend is kicking ass in her battle with breast cancer. Both of my grandmas had cancer. I recently lost a friend to cancer.

Marla Sokoloff

My mom always told me I should have a Plan B. I said that if I'm not going to play guitar I'm going to play drums. And if I'm not going to play drums, I'm going to play bass. I always just wanted to play music. I was completely obsessed.

Gary Clark, Jr.

My mom is in the navy and my dad works for the army, but I never called them 'sir' or 'ma'am' or anything like that, and we never really moved around a lot because both my parents were stationed in D.C.

Ian Harding

Then you've got Georgetown, and I really just like everything about them. When I went down there with my mom, it really opened my eyes to what they were all about. I have to factor in what a school like that can do for me, even away from being a basketball player.

Nerlens Noel

My mom is one of my role models in a complicated way. I learned from her how to be a good mom. She was one of those natural moms who really took to it. Her chosen profession was teaching. She loves kids. But she was extremely frustrated and unhappy because for much of my life she was a stay-at-home mom.

Leslie Morgan Steiner

My parents waited to have me and my sister - my dad was 43 when my mother had me, and my mom was 38. They purposefully waited until they had had their adventures in life so that we wouldn't represent the end of their freedom.

Christian Borle

I was the child who would leave school and take her clothes off the second I got into the house. I made my mom buy me lingerie when I was 5 years old. I was a sicko. My mother must have been mortified.

Alessandra Torresani

There was a modeling agency in my little town where I got my start, but the opportunity came to work in Japan when I was fourteen. My mom went with me until I was seventeen. Her only stipulation was that I had to keep my schoolwork up. My mom was great. She is still my best friend.

Julia Voth

I was brought up bilingual, but there came a point where my mom went back to work and I got a white babysitter, so sadly I lost it. Now I can understand Spanish and put words together, but I don't speak it fluently. I'm ashamed of that.

Michael Trevino

I think our dad and our mom have always told us that in racing we're a team, and we work together, and that's how it's always been, and I think that's how it's always going to be.

Amber Cope

I loved rock and roll when that came in, Bill Haley, Little Richard, Fats Domino, Buddy Holly, Elvis Presley, all those great records. So I begged my mom and dad for a guitar, which eventually they did get me for Christmas, but it went out of tune very quickly, and it hurt my fingers.

Ian McLagan

I have three older brothers, and we all have different combinations of parents. My father was the best man at my mom's first wedding! And my brother's mother - my dad's first wife - is the sister to my mom's first husband's second wife. So my brothers are both stepcousins and stepbrothers. It's very '70s rock.

Inara George

We were never the family that ordered pizza, and my mom never came home with a bucket of fried chicken. My mom always made home-cooked meals. We always sat down at the dinner table as a family.

Haylie Duff

Toronto is a special city, and the environment is perfect for the arts; free and alive. I'm a New Yorker, and Toronto reminds me of a much cleaner New York, so it's like coming home after your mom just cleaned your room for you; for me that's a lovely environment.

Emory Cohen

My father was a soldier. He was a frogman in the special forces in Denmark before I was born, and always the reality of that inspired me. My mom is very left-wing, classic socialist, and she always talked about the solders as almost crazy, violent, sick people, and I want to confront that because its very judgmental, and I'm not sure it's true.

Tobias Lindholm

Because of my unique experience as my mom's child, the beginning of my journey was more about me trying to figure out who I was on my own. My mom is one of the greatest moms and so supportive of all my siblings and of all of us being who we are, and not who she wanted us to be.

Tracee Ellis Ross

My grandmother had six kids - one died as an infant - and she was dirt-poor, and all her kids got an education. And my mom grew up poor. And they both worked so hard and cultivated so much of their own happiness. I wanted to have that like an amulet. Not like armor, but like a magic feather. Like Dumbo's magic feather.

Lucy Alibar

When I was two and a half or three, my mom got a call from someone asking if wanted to go on an audition. I ended up getting the job; it was a commercial for Hasbro. It was my first audition and first commercial. I just had to smile and laugh and dance around.

Megan Charpentier

I grew up watching movies and television, and one day when I was really young I told my mom I wanted to become an actor, and she was really supportive and got me involved in local theater and commercials. From there I moved up to auditioning for movies and television.

Cameron Monaghan

My mom started an air-freight company; my grandmother built a golf course. I have a certain degree of entrepreneurial risk-taking in my family history. Maybe that eventually rubbed off on me a little bit.

Brian Acton

Well I was eight years old, and I have an older cousin who is three years older than me and she was doing acting, commercials, and modeling at the time and... to see my cousin doing that was really inspiring and I wanted to do it. So I went to my mom and I asked her if I could do it, and for the acting part of it, she made me study for a year.

Hailee Steinfeld

In 'Bras & Broomsticks,' Rachel Weinstein gets the shock of her life when she discovers that her mom and her younger sister, Miri, are both... witches! In 'Frogs & French Kisses,' Rachel and her witchy family are back - Miri is busy zapping up ways to save the world, while Mom has gone boy crazy and become a magicaholic.

Sarah Mlynowski

I'm trying hard to keep my Australian accent. My mom would disown me if I didn't.

Maia Mitchell

I don't have a creepy uncle, but I certainly have many, many uncles. My mom has twelve brothers and sisters, and my dad has two sisters and three brothers. Their maturity level is still hovering around fifteen when they all get together, but they're not necessarily creepy.

Martha MacIsaac

I definitely got my philanthropic genes from my mom and dad. They taught me from a very early age to always lend a helping hand to anyone in need, and I hope to raise my daughter to be a very kind and charitable person.

Rebecca Gayheart

I have six brothers and one sister, and I was an ice hockey player when I was younger. I think my dad thought I was going to be in the women's league for ice hockey. But, I totally fell in love with drama in grade school, and I asked my mom if I could get involved with it.

Nicola Peltz

You see people, you judge. It's just the human thing to do - good or bad, it's a fact. Like when you get a coffee at Starbucks and the person is rude to you. My mom always says, 'Yeah, but you don't know what kind of day they're having.' You don't know the back-story, and that's why it's so fun to be an actor and to get into the back-story.

Nicola Peltz

My off-the-field heroes, the people who gave me the values to live by and who inspired me with their hard work and unselfish dedication to their family, were my mom, Catherine, and my dad, William.

Allan Ray

I was four when I started modeling. My mom was very much an off-the-stage mom who knew nothing about the business. She married my stepdad when I was about four, and he had been an actor. Because I was a really smiley kid and could read, which is something they're always looking for, she just decided to give it a shot.

Charlotte Arnold

This is actually something no one knows, but my mom was really the one who created the entire style for 'Teen Witch.' I'm dead serious. She was super involved, and is super creative, so I wore a lot of my actual clothes in the movie. Truly, Louise was my mom's vision. She really created an iconic character.

Robyn Lively

I think that even though my father wasn't there, in his death and in his memory, he has been a mentor to me in my manhood because my mom couldn't teach me how to be a man.

Francis Capra

When I was younger, I had a perm, and it was really big. My mom was a hairdresser, so even my dad had a perm! I looked like a poodle, but it was cool at the time.

Heidi Klum

Fortunately, when you're a mom, the responsibility of caring for your child can keep you going.

Shania Twain

I consider my mom and all my sisters my friends.

Alexa Vega

My mom insisted on multigrain bread and never allowed soda in the house.

Vin Diesel

I watched my parents. My dad worked nights, and I was aware of how much he was doing for us. My mom was a Tupperware lady and also worked at the school. I always felt that I couldn't let them down. And I had a natural discipline from early on. I was always training for something.

Jennifer Lopez

My mom's discipline worked out perfectly. I wouldn't change a thing.

will.i.am

My mom says: 'Why aren't you a doctor?' and I'm like, 'I am a doctor!' and she's all, 'No, I mean a real doctor.' She reads my books, but she says they give her a headache.

Brian Greene

My dad and mom believed that you do what you have to do in private and don't make a big deal out of it. Just try to help people as much as you can.

Harry Connick, Jr.

It's so funny looking back, but my so-called overnight success actually took 15 years. I remember when I didn't have any money, and my only car was mom's Hyundai.

Criss Angel

I love my mom. I totally look up to her, and she just doesn't let anybody take advantage of me. People might call that a stage mom.

Hilary Duff

I remember getting this scrapbook that this girl made, that I actually gave to my mom to hold onto because she has a 'Twilight' shrine in their house in Florida. It was just this scrapbook of me, starting with 'Twilight,' and the whole progression of me and my career throughout that, and other stuff that I had done in between.

Ashley Greene

My memory of my mom is a wine glass in one hand and a cigarette in the other. She was a runway fashion model, and she was quite a glamorous woman.

Loni Anderson

Every single thing I learned about marketing and building my business, I learned from my mom, and she had never been in the workforce. She just had great practical sense.

Barbara Corcoran

My mom kind of led me toward acting. She wanted to be an actress when she was younger. That made me interested in it when I was a kid, because she and I are very close.

Stephen Colbert

If I could be a third of the woman that my mom is and have a third of the strength that she has, then I will have done good by this life.

Brittany Murphy

My mom is like this hard-core, liberal feminist. She's a

professor in Boston, and she's been teaching women's studies for 30 years and international politics.

Eliza Dushku

Every family is different. I am mom and I am dad and I'm going to do my best. You should be proud, walk through life saying I have the coolest family. I am part of a modern family.

Ricky Martin

My mom, she's still always there for me. Always.

David Ortiz

I was born to a single mom and raised by her and my grandparents.

Anthony Foxx

My mom won't let me buy high-fashion stuff unless it's TK Maxx or a birthday occasion.

Chloe Grace Moretz

When I was born, my dad and my mom gave me names,

but in Africa, when your child is born, especially close family members can suggest names they want to add on. Maybe your grandmom and your grandpop have something to add to the name of the child.

Dikembe Mutombo

For a kid who's lost his mom and all the rage and grief that no one was able to talk out of me, football was a very therapeutic sport. Very.

Jon Hamm

My brother Trevor is theatrically trained. I used to watch him when I was younger and I was in love with it. It just seemed really fun to be someone else. So I begged my mom; she was hesitant, but she eventually allowed me. And it turned out well, I guess.

Chloe Grace Moretz

My mom is actually a former prima ballerina, and all the women in my family are associated either with dance or choreography or acting, so I'm very lucky in a way because I grew up in a family of artists. I've been dancing since I was a little kid.

Ksenia Solo

I need my mom for moral support plus to do the house things.

Melky Cabrera

My mom is always with me. When I made my major-league debut I told her, 'That's it. You don't work anymore. I'm going to work and take care of you.'

Melky Cabrera

My father loved 'Godard and Truffaut.' He was more artsy. My mom loved the 'Bourne' trilogy; she likes big blockbusters. She loved that I did 'I Am Legend.' My passion for acting came with my passion for movies.

Alice Braga

I always tell people, I'm a better swimmer because I'm a mom and a better mom because I'm swimmer.

Amanda Beard

My mom and my dad were both very sociable, meeting lots of interesting people.

Bill Gates

America isn't Congress. America isn't Washington. America is the striving immigrant who starts a business, or the mom who works two low-wage jobs to give her kid a better life. America is the union leader and the CEO who put aside their differences to make the economy stronger.

Barack Obama

Any charity that aids or supports trying to find a cure for cancer is very close to my heart. My mom had cancer multiple times, so it's something that I can relate to.

Jennette McCurdy

My dad died when I was young; my mom remarried with more haste than sense to a fellow... he wasn't evil or anything, but he was worthless.

P. J. O'Rourke

I'm too tough and sensitive to have to have some pubescent twerp with his mom's earring in his tongue, who combs his hair with Redi-Whip and has an Ani DiFranco tattoo on his shin, come show me how a computer works.

P. J. O'Rourke

As a mom, I know it is my responsibility, and no one

else's, to raise my kids. But we have to ask ourselves, what does it mean when so many parents are finding their best efforts undermined by an avalanche of advertisements aimed at our kids.

Michelle Obama

When I was a kid, there were no credit cards. Instead, retailers offered layaway plans. My mom would go to a store, such as a furniture outlet, choose the sofa she wanted, and put it on layaway. That meant she put a little money down to hold the sofa, and every payday she'd pay a little toward the purchase.

Robert Kiyosaki

My mom really inspired me. She has always taught me it's not about us, it's about what we can give back.

Bailee Madison

I once went on the most grueling radio tour. Living in hotel rooms, sleeping in the backs of rental cars as my mom drove to three different cities in one day.

Taylor Swift

I'm a real stay-at-home mom. I'm really hands-on.

Everything else became secondary.

Drew Barrymore

Whenever I don't get injured, the film is a dud. I didn't bleed on 'Rhinestone.' I didn't bleed on 'Stop! Or My Mom will Shoot.'

Sylvester Stallone

I never thought I was a great mom. I always worked. I fell in love with my children as they got older.

Marla Gibbs

My mom used to say that Greek Easter was later because then you get stuff cheaper.

Amy Sedaris

When we lived in a suburb of Atlanta, Georgia, my sister and I did a local play. My whole family got involved. My mom did the makeup. My sister and I were being homeschooled, and my parents wanted us to be socialized. We had a lot of fun with the other kids hanging out backstage.

Danielle Panabaker

My question about luging is, How do you get into the luge community to begin with? Is it one day like, 'Mom, Dad, I really want to luge.' And your parents are like: 'O.K., I'll quit my job. We'll move to an Alpine community.'

Douglas Coupland

My mom lived with me until I started making enough money to support myself. I was asking her to leave the entire time. I'd been ready to move out since I was, like, 14.

Megan Fox

Every single second of every single day... I don't know if I feel like a bad mom, but at the end of the day I'm always plagued with, 'Did I do enough? Should I go in a different direction?'

Sandra Bullock

I became a mom at 37 and having a child has been an emancipation for me.

Tori Amos

My mom was tough.

Tiger Woods

I did say that I wanted to be a young mom, just because my mom was a young mom. It is better because I can be closer to my kids and stuff.

Lindsay Lohan

I wish I had an extra day with my mom sometimes. Or another hour in the day with my family, husband and children.

Mary J. Blige

I'm frugal. I've always been this way. When I was young, my mom would give me my allowance, and I'd peel off a little each week and have some to spare.

Tyra Banks

My mom was a medical photographer, but on the side, she did a before-and-after glam photography business in the house. She would do makeup and hair - and I was her assistant.

Tyra Banks

I lived with my mom in a really small apartment. My bedroom was like in the living room. That's why I still love to sleep on couches now.

Alicia Keys

My mom, if you asked her if she was interested in whether or not people gambled, would say no.

Penn Jillette

It is a sad commentary of our times when our young must seek advice and counsel from 'Dear Abby' instead of going to Mom and Dad.

Pauline Phillips

My mom's hot. I mean she's old, but my mom's out of control.

Paul Walker

When I was younger, I wouldn't speak up as much, but now that I'm a mom, things have changed.

Britney Spears

I have spoken honestly about being born into a home where there was discord and chaos. I saw my mom have a rough time with my dad being very controlling, which is why I push back whenever I feel like someone is trying to box me in. It makes me run for the hills.

Christina Aguilera

I know I'm talented, but I wasn't put here to sing. I was put here to be a wife and a mom and look after my family. I love what I do, but it's not where it begins and ends.

Amy Winehouse

My mom was my main influence growing up, and Phylicia Rashad reminded me a lot of my mother, just the way she handled certain things, she was... not soft-spoken but smooth-spoken. Just very calm, cool, collected about things.

Queen Latifah

Mom was the greatest influence of my childhood. She wanted to save me from the vice, lust, and drinking that was all about me.

Ethel Waters

I barely saw my mother, and the mom I saw was often angry and unhappy. The mother I grew up with is not the mother I know now. It's not the mother she became after my father died, and that's been the greatest prize of my life.

Sonia Sotomayor

I was born and raised in East Los Angeles by a single mom who had three biological kids and adopted four more. I never met my dad.

will.i.am

My parents split up when I was young, and I was living with my mom for a little while, then I was kind of just on my own really young. It wasn't some kind of global tragedy, it was just never really a very close-knit family. So there was support in the sense that they didn't stand in my way.

Ani DiFranco

My mom obviously had a problem.

Dave Pelzer

When I was a little girl, rocking my little dolls, I remember thinking I would be the world's best mom, and so far I've done it.

Jenny McCarthy

She had a hit for every syllable: 'Don't. You. Ever. Talk. To. Me. Like. That. Ever. Again.' That was the last time I ever talked back to Mom.

Misty May-Treanor

My mom had Julia Child and 'The Fannie Farmer Cookbook' on top of the refrigerator, and she had a small repertoire of French dishes.

Anthony Bourdain

Yes, I always remember my dad's, mom's and my grandma's perfumes.

Marc Jacobs

I came from a broken home, so my mom was a major influence in my life.

Julius Erving

My mom was a ventriloquist and she always was throwing her voice. For ten years I thought the dog was telling me to kill my father.

Wendy Liebman

I don't drink, and I don't smoke. It's a personal preference. My mom has never drunk or smoked. I look up to my mom.

Ashley Tisdale

I've always wanted to be sure my parents approve of what I do. Even with my tattoos, my mom went with me.

Ashley Tisdale

My dad is a Deadhead, my mom's a Jewish-American princess from Jersey.

Adam Lambert

My mother told me Homer Ditto was not my father. Nope. Mom had had a fling with some other guy who was my dad. Some dude who didn't stick around too long who Mom was happy to get rid of. She chose Homer, and Homer chose me, so he lent me his name even though I didn't have his blood.

Beth Ditto

My relationship with my mom is really the single most profound relationship that I've ever had in my life.

Mindy Kaling

I can honestly say, after talking about my mom passing away, I got the biggest weight off of my chest. Comedy is my therapy. That's how I deal with my problems, my personal battles. I talk about it. I give it to my fans. When they laugh at it, it's a release, for lack of a better word.

Kevin Hart

I have great faith that Heaven's there and I'll see my brothers and my mom and dad when I get there.

Ernie Harwell

I would say that my role model, as far as just somebody leading by example, which to me is what a great youth counselor does - they are there to talk to and lead by example - would be my mom, but she wasn't a youth counselor. She was a teacher, and she is a good person and definitely one of the biggest influences in my life.

Carrie Underwood

The only reason I felt like I could sing a song like 'Blown Away' is because I have definitely lived through my fair share of trips to the cellar in the spring. We were no stranger to that. I still ask my mom, 'Is the cellar cleaned out now? Is everything OK?' Even in my new house, I had something built in it that's like a storm shelter.

Carrie Underwood

I got blessed from my mom. She's the personality; she's the one who smiled, so I took on part of her, and who also wanted to help and save the world. Then I took on part of my dad, who is tough.

Magic Johnson

I remember that at the beginning of the month, the kind of menus my mom and father would prepare for us would have fish, chicken. But at the end of the month - because my father would be waiting for paycheck - the refrigerator would get empty. I remember that without a lot of food left, some of the best meals happened right there.

Jose Andres Puerta

I'm ridiculous in my oversharing; my mom and sister are very open but a little more judicious than me... and my father is a decidedly private person.

Lena Dunham

Wigs have always been a part of my life and have become a staple accessory in my closet. I can remember being a little girl and hearing all the commotion in my house from my mom, aunts and grandmother when picking out their wigs for the day. It was such a good time for them and part of their everyday beauty routine.

Sherri Shepherd

The 'believe' tattoo is because my mom always told me to believe.

Ashley Tisdale

I have so much respect for my mom and all the women across the world.

Jessica Simpson

In 2002 Mom and I got a chance to act together in a play called 'Pitching to the Star,' with her brother, Robert Lipton. The three of us on the same stage - that was such a special experience for me.

Rashida Jones

Your mom was right when she told you never to discuss politics and religion because emotions run so high in those arenas. Especially religion.

Bill O'Reilly

My mom's never been married. I've never even seen my mom kiss a dude.

will.i.am

When I got into junior high school, that's when my mom let me dress how I wanted to dress. Up to that point I wore suits to school all the time.

will.i.am

Financial hardships were rough on us, even though Mom had a good job at G.M.

Ryan White

Everything you see is filtered through your visual system (imperfect) and your brain (also imperfect, despite what your mom told you). Witness testimony is the worst kind of evidence in science.

Seth Shostak

When you can impress your mom by saying you've been to someone's concert, you know you're pretty lame.

Gillian Jacobs

I'm not a mom, but I think the word 'mother' is about wisdom.

Margaret Cho

My mom knows when something is real and something is not.

Christina Ricci

My mom lived by herself with two kids. Sacrifice was the name of the game at our house.

Victor Cruz

I learned to hear silence. That's the kind of life I lived: simple. I learned to see things in people around me, in my mom, dad, brothers and sisters.

Sidney Poitier

Washington has got to, across the board, lower taxes for small businesses so that our mom and pops can reinvest and hire people, so that our businesses can thrive.

Sarah Palin

My mom is painfully sweet; she's from Nebraska.

Gabrielle Union

My youngest sister, Cindy, has Down syndrome, and I remember my mother spending hours and hours with her, teaching her to tie her shoelaces on her own, drilling multiplication tables with Cindy, practicing piano every day with her. No one expected Cindy to get a Ph.D.! But my mom wanted her to be the best she could be, within her limits.

Amy Chua

I felt there was a lot of love in my house. And my mom was, you know, the basis of all that.

Joe Torre

I'll tell you, Liz Cheney is going to be a very good candidate. I worked with her during the Bush campaigns. She's smart, she's focused, she's disciplined - and she's got a great back story. She's got a large family. She's a great mom. And she's a hard worker. I think she's going to be a very effective campaigner.

Mark McKinnon

When I decided that I might want to do acting for a living - I don't know where it really came from, since there was no school play or any of that - my mom gave me her blessing. I had to get a scholarship - that was the only way I could have gone to drama school.

Gary Oldman

I remember when I was 11, I told my mom, 'One day I'm going to buy you a house.' And she said, 'Boy, don't you be making promises you can't keep.' I was like: 'No, Ma, it's not a promise. I'm going to buy you a house one day.'

will.i.am

My nickname for my mom was 'The Compass.'

Dane Cook

I didn't know my Dad - he moved out early. And my mom's politics were kind of hardscrabble. She didn't think about Democrats or Republicans. She thought about who made sense. I've been both in my life.

Dennis Miller

My mom is a constant in my life in so many ways.

Kerri Walsh

Dad and mom would have preferred that I be a doctor, a lawyer, a scientist, or a great humanitarian.

Levon Helm

My father moved to Hawaii from Brooklyn and my mother came there as a child from the Philippines. They met at a show where my dad was playing percussion. My mom was a hula dancer.

Bruno Mars

I never get to go to movies, because I'm a mom.

Tina Fey

I had to take my makeup off at work every night. I wasn't allowed to do it at home because my mom said that when your work day is done, you're done with work.

Jodie Foster

My kids haven't watched one episode of 'Growing Pains'. I'll tell you why. When our kids were little, we never wanted Mommy or Daddy to be the celebrity mom or dad to our kids.

Kirk Cameron

My mom, God rest her soul - she liked nicknames. In the womb she named me Skip. There was another black guy in Piedmont, W.Va., and his name was Skip. They called him Big Skip, and I was Little Skip.

Henry Louis Gates

The way my family always did Christmas was on Christmas Eve, it wasn't really centered around a dinner on Christmas Eve. It was more about keeping the kids calm. Sometime after dark is when we were going to open all the presents underneath the tree from Mom, Dad and the kids and everything - just the family presents was every Christmas Eve.

Blake Shelton

The relationship between Cathy and Mom in the strip is the one relationship drawn from real life that I have proudly never even tried to disguise.

Cathy Guisewite

My dad sold encyclopedias and my mom worked in a factory office.

Mike Myers

I have great genes. Thank you to my mom and dad for that one.

Gloria Estefan

I remember going with my mom to a random garage sale as a kid and thinking what a cool treasure hunt that whole world was. Only to transition as an adult to think, 'What a gross place that really is.'

Will Ferrell

I like to work. The self-esteem and satisfaction that I get from working makes me a better person, which makes me a better mom. I feel lucky because I have the luxury of working only one or two days a week.

Cindy Crawford

When it comes to children, my mom doesn't believe in borders. She loves all children, and that's a good example of mothering the world. I need to do that, but before I can, I need to get over my fear of kids in the first place.

Margaret Cho

I was always with a single mom, and we never had schedules or anything. We were just Bohemian, us against the world, which was kind of great, but it certainly didn't breed security. I've gotten hyper-sensitive to schedules and bath time and eating at the dinner table. We don't just 'Bohemian' go out at nine o'clock and go get Chinese food.

Brooke Shields

There are days when I struggle with wanting to be a full-time, stay-at-home mom, and feeling guilty about that because I work.

Tori Spelling

With my new venture, Club Mom, we want to empower moms to feel their value and also build their collective power to make their lives better and easier. We want to bring them together as a community to share experiences and information.

Andrew Shue

My mom was a saint. She taught me to be terminally nice.

Iggy Pop

If my Dad doesn't like you, you will know. My Mom is just too innocent to ever lie. She doesn't even cuss.

Channing Tatum

I have an amazing social-media wing man who manages my Facebook fan site. All my blogs get copied there. My e-mail in-box exploded, and I don't have that kind of time. My mom and sister have their whole life on Facebook, and I'm not there.

Jason Mraz

I listened to the radio, so I was influenced by everyone from Michael Jackson to Milli Vanilli. But thankfully my dad had a collection of Cat Stevens albums while my mom was listening to jazz.

Jason Mraz

I guess now that I think back, I used to play priest and be a funny priest. I don't know, I grew up in such a Catholic family that I kind of liked to test the boundaries a little bit and I think I had fun watching my mom laugh.

Jenny McCarthy

My mom listened to the Beatles and Elvis, a lot of different types of music.

Travis Barker

No matter what, like, I couldn't - I could break a world record, get an Olympic gold medal, and my mom would be, like, you could have done better. But you looked pretty. That's what she says all the time.

Ryan Lochte

My mom was paranoid about my safety.

Jane Smiley

My mom and dad met at Anaheim High School. After they got married, all they wanted to do was have four children, and they did.

Gwen Stefani

I don't have anything against my mom, but my family has no emotional connection to each other.

Adam Carolla

It's been very hard, after being mostly a mom, to develop an adult life of my own. And not being married anymore, I have to come up with challenges.

Danielle Steel

Grades were important in our house. I was reading by two. My mom would sit there and read with me, read with me, read with me. It was wonderful.

Fergie

My dad is like a cactus - introverted and tough. I'm a people person, like my mom, but I got my competitiveness from my dad. He came to this country from Belarus with nothing and built a real business. He's my hero for giving me that need to run a business and for having enormous confidence in me.

Gary Vaynerchuk

Having children is a huge responsibility, and I just don't want to hand them off to a nanny or my mom to take care of them.

Thalia

So far I'm not surprised by anything about being a mom. It's all pretty great - but that's what I expected.

Charlize Theron

My mom was really vigorous about making sure that we saw things and that we questioned things. Education was so important to both of my parents.

Jennifer Garner

Something my mom taught me when I was little is that everything happens for a reason.

Shawn Johnson

Country was about character. Country's changed because of monsters like Clear Channel who bought up all the stations and sliced them up into formats. Our demographic is now the soccer mom.

Gary Allan

My parents separated when I was eight. I grew up with my mom alone.

Julian Casablancas

My mom allowed me to take an old burlap bag and fill it with moss, corn stalks and rocks, then hang it from a tree and spend an hour a day punching my heavy bag.

Joe Frazier

All four of my grandparents were educators, my mom was a school nurse, and I went through the public school system.

Erin Cummings

Imagine my surprise when, after a lifetime of teaching me to keep personal things to myself, Mom insisted my drawings were the start of a comic strip for millions of people to enjoy.

Cathy Guisewite

I'm a mom, so I have to be comfortable. Jeans are a staple - I have way too many in my closet! It's warm in Florida, so I wear jeans and a tank top every day. I love my True Religions, my Rich and Skinny, and Citizens of Humanity. But I also love getting dressed up!

Candace Cameron Bure

My mom is a really good cook. I didn't get the cooking gene, but she cooks this really amazing dinner every Christmas, and that's always really fun.

Miranda Cosgrove

My food is Louisiana, New Orleans-based, well-seasoned, rustic. I think it's pretty unique because of my background being influenced by my mom, Portuguese and French Canadian. There's a lot going on there.

Emeril Lagasse

I grew up painting and playing piano so when I was a little kid I thought I was going to be an artist or a painter but my mom had me taking piano lessons for about 10-12 years as a young kid.

Mike Shinoda

People who build family businesses are not classically trained. They have to deal with an enormous amount of politics. You think corporate politics are tough? Go work for your dad or your mom.

Gary Vaynerchuk

I'm from Tennessee. My mom lives in Nashville. I'm born and bred country. That's all I listen to.

Lucy Hale

I am proud of my kids, but I also want to make my mom proud of me. I'm still a momma's girl at the heart of the situation.

Tori Spelling

I'm a military kid, both parents in the military - Mom did 12 years, Dad did 21, served in two wars. So discipline is something that was huge.

Robert Griffin III

I love my mom and dad.

Taylor Momsen

Home is where my mom is.

Brittany Murphy

My mom would always read a book to me at night from when I was three. Now, I can't go to sleep without reading a book. At the same time, once I read, it's difficult for me to go to sleep, as I have an overactive imagination and I start thinking.

Sonam Kapoor

Reading has made me more open, has improved my understanding, and has made me a better artiste, but it also makes me live in my own bubble. My mom keeps asking me, 'What do you read in that room the whole day?' Once I am into a book, I will finish it.

Sonam Kapoor

When I watch my kids, and I see the primal level at which the sibling relationships are formed, then I completely understand what these unresolved adult sibling problems are based on. You know, 'Mom liked you better' and, 'You got your own room and I didn't.'

Annette Bening

My father's a deacon, my mother's a choir director, so I grew up in the church and singing in the choir, begging my mom if I could have a solo.

Keke Palmer

I guess my mom raised me right. She was very celebratory of her body. I never heard her once say, 'I feel fat.'

Christina Hendricks

My mom taught me not to talk about money.

Hilary Duff

I was labeled a troublemaker, my mom an unfit mother, and I was not welcome anywhere.

Ryan White

No, my mom kind of led me toward acting. She wanted to be an actress when she was younger. That made me interested in it when I was a kid, because she and I are very close.

Stephen Colbert

I wanted to be a 150% entrepreneur and a 150% mom, and I found that I was having a very hard time doing both. I was about 75% and 75% - still better than 100%, but not what I was accustomed to at work.

Barbara Corcoran

I was a sickly baby, and after two sets of adoptive parents took me home, they returned me to the orphanage because of a serious respiratory infection. But as they say, the third time's a charm, because my mom and dad adopted me and took me into their home where I was raised in a family full of love.

Rodney Atkins

I'm not a doctor or scientist. I'm just a mom. But I do think there's a genetic predisposition, and there are environmental triggers. I feel like that combination, in my child's case, is what resulted in autism.

Holly Robinson Peete

My wife was born and raised in Italy until she was about 9, and then she came to America, and her mom was a great cook, and they have great recipes, and whenever her mom would come into town, we would have all these friends just randomly showing up at our house, and eventually we figured out why. They wanted Mama's cooking.

Bill Rancic

My mom has never been a big meddler and isn't, like, extremely opinionated or at least just doesn't voice it to me. She's sort of let me come into my own by myself, and I think that's just a testament to what my parents did in terms of raising us.

Mandy Moore

My mom's one of 13 siblings, and they all got six kids, and till I was 13 everybody was in Compton.

Kendrick Lamar

My mom makes the best Cajun stuff. I'm a big gumbo guy. I've lost a lot of my Louisiana accent, so now when I say 'gumbo,' I feel like someone who's never said the word before.

Hunter Hayes

My mom's a social worker, and my dad works in non-profit organisations.

Seth Rogen

The Chinese mom is not the helicopter mom. I would never do their homework for them. It's all about: Take responsibility, don't blame others. Be self-reliant. Never blame the teacher.

Amy Chua

I'm not one of those Hollywood moms where my kid is three weeks old and I'm a size zero. I'm a real woman and I'm a working woman and a working mom.

Kimora Lee Simmons

My mom and my father's birthday are on the same day.

Victor Cruz

I did not have a father. It was my mom who chose to be alone. She felt that she would be better off by herself with me after I was born.

Olga Kurylenko

Trying to be Supermom is as futile as trying to be Perfect Mom. Not going to happen.

Arianna Huffington

I've learned that every working mom is a superwoman.

Uma Thurman

I come from labor country. My mom was a teacher and was very involved in the teachers' union.

John Wells

So, I remember when I was a kid, I was waiting for my mom to come home when she was working late, and, you know, I was like, 'Oh my God, what happened to her? Is she OK? Did something happen to her getting in the car?' I was a little kid. But those are actually early onsets of anxiety.

Vinny Guadagnino

It's impossible to put yourself first when you're a mom.

Jillian Michaels

Mom claimed that I could carry a tune at 2 or 3 years of age. Maybe she was a little prejudiced.

Ethel Merman

My mom did costumes for the Pointer Sisters.

Slash

I lived in small town out in the desert and my friend used to steal his mom's car in the middle of the night. He'd drive over to my house, I'd sneak out and we'd go out to the desert and just burn things down.

Mark Hoppus

I was almost 8 years old when I was watching a kid on a TV commercial, and I told my mom that I wanted to do the same thing. She said that I would need to get an agent and that she would research it.

Victoria Justice

I have a very broad demographic, from the 8-year-old who knows every word to 'Ice Ice Baby' and the college kid who grew up on 'Ninja Rap' to the soccer mom and grandparent.

Vanilla Ice

When I was 7, I came up with the idea of 'charm socks.' My mom would take me to buy bags of plastic charms, we would sew them on frilly white socks, and I sold them at school.

Sara Blakely

My mom was a professional. My dad and mom met each other in a movie called 'New Faces of 1937.' My mom went under the name Thelma Leeds, and she did a few movies, and she was really a great singer, and when she married my dad and started to have a family, she sang at parties.

Albert Brooks

I had massive anxiety as a child. I was in therapy. From 8 to 10, I was borderline agora-phobic. I could not leave my mom's side. I don't really have panic attacks anymore, but I had really bad anxiety.

Emma Stone

When I was 15, I worked at a dry cleaner because I wanted Abercrombie & Fitch jeans. My mom told me I could have $20 jeans, not $70 jeans, unless I was willing to work for them. So I did!

Ashley Greene

I know not every mom is a secret KGB spy, but every

mom has this whole other life. Every dad and every person has this whole other life.

Keri Russell

My mom was on welfare and the occasional food stamp, but I have never participated in any of those governmental programs, even the ones that kind of work like education, scholarships and whatever, and I managed to do just fine.

Adam Carolla

I've had to adapt my wardrobe to my various roles, both at the office, as a mom, and for television. When I shop for the season I look for pieces that will suit every facet of my daily life, not just one single occasion.

Nina Garcia

My mom taught me German before I knew English. And I went to French immersion school.

Tatiana Maslany

My dad was the one who really loved basketball, and he was the one that put the basketball in my hands, and my mom was 'Team Mom' of all my teams. I used to play for three or four teams at once and she would just spend her entire afternoon driving me from practice to practice to practice.

Jeremy Lin

I spend my afternoons painting and working on my Open Hearts jewelry line for Kay Jewelers. I designed an image of a heart that isn't completely closed. My mom always told me to live with an open heart - when life gets tough, you should go out and help someone else.

Jane Seymour

I was two years old when my mom put me in mommy and me classes. I always had a lot of energy so it was the perfect fit!

Aly Raisman

I've always eaten egg whites because when I was little, I didn't like the color yellow, so my mom would trick me into eating eggs by taking out the yolk.

Eva Longoria

I've had broken bones and cuts and dashes and tears from movies, but when I was five, my mom put the biscuits up high so we wouldn't be helping ourselves. So, one day I asked to stand up on a chair to get a biscuit, and it fell, and the corner of the chair went right into the side of my eye, and it made a big hole in there.

Gerard Butler

In all honesty, at that time, I never saw myself as an author... I was just a Mom in a state of panic, trying to enter a short story contest to win the prize money in order to keep the lights on in my home.

Leslie Banks

Well, my mom taught public school music for almost 40 years. And she's about 5 feet - and very mighty. And she would control her kids a lot by giving them the eye, or the stare.

Vanessa Williams

Being a working mom, you want to make a difference in our schools, which is making a difference in our children and ultimately it's making a difference in our community.

Kimora Lee Simmons

My dad was a Punjabi from Amritsar, and my mom is a Punjabi from Kashmir. My dad was a soldier in the Indian

Army.

Akshay Kumar

My mom used to have a lot of European cinema playing in the house, so I'd catch bits and pieces of films.

Mia Wasikowska

My parents divorced when I was young but I was brought up in two really loving households. I didn't have a contentious relationship with my mom or dad.

Matt Damon

There is nothing like becoming a mom to fill you with fear.

Arianna Huffington

My Mom always cooked healthy. Greek food lends itself to cooking healthy.

Cat Cora

My original inspiration was my mom: a few years after the death of my dad, she started dating one my teachers!

Meg Cabot

My mom was always the support. I can always go out to her and she'll always find the positive in things.

Caroline Wozniacki

I care so passionately about improving the quality of life for women and girls, not just here in the United States, but internationally as well. I am a single mom and I raised a daughter who is now a young adult.

Valerie Jarrett

Realizing you're not anything special to the kids is always a great sort of reminder that you're just a regular person. A regular, embarrassing old mom.

Reese Witherspoon

A company that pays attention to the family unit is a successful company. We don't isolate the family. We don't make rides that say, 'Hey mom, dad, you go sit on the bench.'

Michael Eisner

I like to write and draw and paint, and my mom's an artist, so I think I get caught up in thinking, 'I'm afraid it's gonna be bad,' and it's hard for me to start sometimes.

Kristen Wiig

My mom and my dad wanted my brother and I to have a better life, you know, better education, better jobs. It was probably harder, much, much harder, for my parents. When you're a kid, you can learn a language much more easily; I learned English in less than a year.

Mila Kunis

It scared my mom to death when all my friends started driving. She always told me she wanted me to drive, but I think she kind of felt lucky that I didn't get my permit when all my friends did. I think that's been the hardest thing for her, watching me go out with my friends and literally drive away.

Miranda Cosgrove

My mom was scared of the old Times Square so I was never allowed to go. Now I'm scared of the new Times Square, so I still never go.

Padma Lakshmi

Being a mom's so empowering and incredible. I'm one of those people who believes that life brings things to you at a certain time for a certain reason, and if you just go with it, that's where the best moments come from.

Ashlee Simpson

My parents got divorced when I was around a year old. My dad was essentially a nonentity in my life until I got to be about 16 or so. My mom was a flight attendant for PanAm, so I moved all over the world. London, Rio de Janeiro.

Tucker Max

My mom and dad just loved the fact that I fooled around. They just embraced it. They'd always kind of enjoy it, and they liked it when I made them laugh.

Dominic Monaghan

You need your mom and dad to protect you. It means they love you so much.

Gabby Douglas

I have no ties to my dad. I had no communications with him; it didn't shape who I am or anything like that. I'm actually a product of my mom.

M.I.A.

I think 'Actions speak louder than words' is one thing, I think, I always took from my mom. And to this day, I think about that in everything I do.

Ginni Rometty

You have a dream 35 years ago - doesn't come to fruition, but you move on with life. But it's somewhere back there. Then you turn 60, and your mom just dies, and you're looking for something. And the dream comes waking out of your imagination.

Diana Nyad

Learn to expect less from life and more from yourself. Accept the changes that life throws at you. Remember, your destiny is pretty much in your hands. So, as your mom may have told you, keep them clean.

Lynda Resnick

I always wanted to be a young mom, but generations of women have worked so hard so we can have a career and wait to have children. So I say carpe diem - take advantage of that.

Brittany Murphy

When I was 11 my friend's mom made a peanut butter sandwich. I ate the sandwich and was like, 'I'm never eating anything else again.' And I still eat peanut butter every day. I would put peanut butter on a steak.

Aasif Mandvi

I've always had a sick sense of humor, and I've always wanted that to permeate the music because I don't take myself seriously. I take the music seriously, but I know I'm not God's gift to anyone except my mom.

Josh Homme

I wasn't one to go out and buy a new car and stereo system and expensive clothes. My mom helped keep me grounded.

Christina Applegate

My mom grew up in poverty in Oklahoma - like Dust Bowl, nine people in one room kind of place - and the way she got out of poverty was through education. My dad grew up without a dad, with very little and he also made his way out through education.

Jennifer Garner

I love what I do and I think it shows. As my kids get older, they can see me as a mom who loves working.

Jessica Capshaw

I'm a pretty tenacious person; I get that from my mom. So sometimes, I use dark humor. I can't take myself too seriously.

Art Alexakis

'Peace Mom' is my most heartfelt, but I am most proud of 'Myth America' because I nailed the problem and gave the solutions long before the Occupy Movement. I think it's a great organic class analysis.

Cindy Sheehan

The military infrastructure grew me. My faith in God is important, my belief in my country is important, my relationship to my family is important, the things that Mom and Dad tell you growing up are important.

Tommy Franks

You need a strong family because at the end, they will love you and support you unconditionally. Luckily, I have my dad, mom and sister.

Esha Gupta

My mom and I used to listen to records, read, and take train rides across the country in the summer. It was a very chill life. She didn't expose me to anything that was ahead of my development, but she expected me to adjust to her world - she did not expect to adjust to mine.

Martha Plimpton

I told my mom I would graduate. I owe that much to her and myself.

Carmelo Anthony

The most inspiring piece of advice I've gotten is simply to persevere. My mom taught me to always keep going no matter what from an early age. When it feels too difficult to push forward, I always remind myself, 'This too shall pass,' and then I redouble my efforts.

Liya Kebede

My mom's a translator, my dad's a woodworker; that's the

world I grew up in, that's the world I'm most comfortable in. The whole idea of Hollywood or any of that other stuff that unfortunately goes along with film, that wasn't part of my upbringing, thankfully.

Tatiana Maslany

My mom grew up in Idaho, went to Brigham Young University: they're very Molly Mormon. And my father is, like, first generation Albanian, and his parents lived in Southey and grew up in downtown Boston. My parents are complete opposites.

Eliza Dushku

My mom is a painter and photographer and my grandfather was an artist, so I've always been surrounded by creative people.

Dylan Lauren

My mom put me in a Pampers commercial on TV.

Christian Slater

I didn't choose 'Silver Spoons'. I think my mom and agent chose it because at that time there was a lack of patience on some of the people that were in charge of my career. I think there was a big offer on the table, and I think they took it.

Ricky Schroder

I deal with postpartum feelings by reaching out to mom friends. I became very close with some of the women in my prenatal yoga class.

Alyssa Milano

I did a movie called 'Quicksand No Escape' with Donald Sutherland and Tim Matheson. I think I was maybe 5. I was really little. Yeah, it was fun. And actually, Felicity Huffman played my mom.

Kaley Cuoco

All of the reality TV I've done has usually been simultaneously an opportunity to create awareness or raise funds for my mom's breast cancer organization.

Stephen Baldwin

My mom is a sculptress.

P. J. Harvey

My dad is a chemical engineer, and my mom was a teacher. They were pretty serious about education, but I always thought about things a little bit differently.

Aaron Levie

I feel such a sense of empowerment being a mom. But I do wonder: How do they/we do it all?

Kourtney Kardashian

I love being at home now, improving my cooking. I've got a really bad memory, so my first attempts were a disaster - I'd forget what ingredients to put in. But I do a lasagna that's a crowd-pleaser, and a good lemon drizzle cake, which I take to my mom's for the Sunday roast to fatten the family up.

Katy B

Death can't be so bad if mom went through it. It makes it easier for the child to follow.

Danny Aiello

If you don't have savings, and your co-founders are as poor as you are, and if Mom and Dad won't loan you money, then your best bet is to find people that know you - your friends. If they, too, won't help, then you're stuck seeking out angel investors.

Vivek Wadhwa

My mom is an art teacher and is very much into the performing arts. What can I say? She is the female in my life and has guided me on how to act and conduct myself. A lot of my strength comes from her.

Erin Andrews

I'm like any working mom.

Kelly Ripa

They wrapped her up like a baby burrito to show to Mom. Here were a mother and her daughter and I love them both so much. I couldn't wait for Courtney to come to the hospital so I could have all my women together.

Al Roker

I always had short hair, and I hated my short hair. I was always mistaken for a boy, but my mom wouldn't let me change my hair because she was always chasing me around with a hairbrush, and it was always tangled, so she just would cut it off, and she's right: short hair did suit me.

Dorothy Hamill

My dad was a good athlete. My mom had longevity. There were some athletic genes that certainly got passed down.

Hale Irwin

My dad is a successful television producer, director and writer and my mom's a director and writer.

Troian Bellisario

My mom, she's a breast cancer survivor and because of that I had started getting mammograms once a year, starting at age 30.

Kate Walsh

My mom and my dad are ebullient people, and I think I carry that with me.

Michael Stuhlbarg

As someone who has been both a full-time mom and full-time in work force, I know we all have valuable experiences that shape who we are.

Teresa Heinz

When I was 7, an old lady was driving too fast in my neighborhood and hit me with her car. I was running out of the house, and when I got halfway into the street, my mom saw the car and yelled for me to run back. As I turned around the car hit me, dragged me five houses down the road, and I fractured my collarbone.

Rutina Wesley

While I circled around and around in my brown rental skates, I studied a group of skaters spinning in the center. I was fascinated! When my mom picked me up, I began a campaign for skating lessons.

Gracie Gold

Some of the best times I've spent in Colorado have been in the backcountry with my mom and siblings, and more recently, with my own kids. That is why I'm concerned to see today's kids spending more time browsing the Internet than exploring nature.

Mark Udall

I love the surprise element of being a mom.

Jessica Capshaw

In Australia, I can just say to my mom, 'I'm going down the street.' And I can walk around pretty much all the places I know.

Kodi Smit-McPhee

When I was growing up in New Jersey, my mom would regularly take my sister and I into the city to see shows. I have many fond memories of standing in the half-price ticket line in Times Square and going to matinees.

Trey Anastasio

My mom, the fabulous Bertie Kinsey, is an amazing seamstress. She quilts and sews and is so crafty. We call her the Southern Martha Stewart!

Angela Kinsey

A small gold plain cross was passed down from my grandma to my mom, then to me, and now to my daughter. It is always nice to own something that connects you to the women who made it possible for you to exist.

Liya Kebede

I'm a mom. I'm from Ethiopia. I gave birth in the U.S. and had all the proper care available to me. If I had given birth in Ethiopia - I don't know if I might have even survived it.

Liya Kebede

I got to say 'Hi' to Dolly Parton, which my mom thought was kind of cool.

Landon Donovan

For a long time, I refused to wear jeans. I liked high-waisted pants, but jeans made me feel like I wasn't being unique. Even now, I won't wear the skinny-jeans style, because most people wear those - they have to be baggier, boyfriend-looking, or sort of like a mom jean. I'm real funny that way.

Elle Fanning

I couldn't wait until I grew up. I used to look at my mom's stockings and put them on with her high heels and mess with my hair.

Florence Griffith Joyner

Mom and I often talked about the trip we'd someday take together to the 'city of eternal spring' where she was born. In Kunming, she said, the fruits are sweeter, the mountains look like Chinese paintings, and the weather is always perfect.

Tess Gerritsen

My parents had five children in six years and one week, meaning that my mom was pregnant for most of the '60s and driving carpools for most of the '70s. When we were young, she dressed us alike so she could pick us out in crowds: identical skirts for the four girls with the color-coordinated pants for my brother.

Christine Pelosi

I snap with my mom. It was a great way for me to see my dog when I was in college. We send selfies, too.

Evan Spiegel

My whole life sort of ended when my mom died.

Cheryl Strayed

I love New York. I first came here with my Mom when I was in 9th grade. I took the subway for the first time and the doors closed between me and my Mom, and I was so scared. I could see her through the window and I didn't know what to do. I got off at the next stop and she caught up to me, but I couldn't stop crying.

Skylar Grey

As a mom, I always feel I have to protect them. I talk about them because they are the most important things in my life but they are private people. I won't use them for my own press.

Jami Gertz

I finished high school, moved to Nashville for college, and set out to break into the music business. Every night when I called home with news of my experiences, my mom and dad would encourage me to keep taking those small steps.

Trisha Yearwood

Being a child that grew up with a single mom back in the '70s, Father's Day to me was always a very uncomfortable time. At school, we would make Father's Day cards for our dads, and I usually mailed one to my dad, and he hardly ever responded.

Art Alexakis

When I was a kid, I played sports a lot. My mom and dad were divorced, but I hung out in the neighborhood a lot, and it was all about sports. I would be out all day on the sand lot or on the hockey rink. My dad would take me to baseball games, but he worked so hard, and he would always fall asleep.

Alex Gibney

My dad's name is Vernon and my mom liked the initials, V. V. My sisters and I got named Victoria, Valerie and Vincent so we'd be V. V.'s, too. But, then when you start getting pets' names that start with a 'v,' it's a little embarrassing.

Vince Vaughn

My mom used to call me a parrot, because the way I spoke would change in every country we'd go to.

Hannah Simone

I grew up with the classics. My mom and I would sit and watch 'Singin' in the Rain' and 'White Christmas' - those kind of movies.

Lucas Grabeel

Mom still has a huge, beautifully decorated Christmas tree. The whole family comes together after midnight mass and has the traditional plum cake and wine. We spend the night at mom's home, and in the morning we wake up and open the presents. In the afternoon, we sit down to have a traditional Christmas lunch.

Malaika Arora Khan

Luckily, I discovered ice skating when I was eight and a half years old. There were two wonderful ponds within walking distance of my house. After all the physical activity the summer provided, I craved movement in the cold of winter. I had no skates, so Mom stuffed socks into my brother's old ones.

Dorothy Hamill

My goal is to be a household name, and when I do that, I want to help other girls become models, and maybe even launch a fashion line with my mom, like Beyonce did with her mother. My mom has such a good eye, and it's always been a dream of hers.

Chanel Iman

I think my mom threatened to put me up for adoption a few times.

Ivanka Trump

Being an only child, I didn't have any other family but my mom and dad really, since the rest of my family lived quite far away from London.

Tom Hardy

My own back yard, and my mom and dad's back yard, is where I learned about tomatoes and weeds and daily maintenance.

John Bytheway

Statistics are to baseball what a flaky crust is to Mom's apple pie.

Harry Reasoner

I'm blessed because I had my mom as a teacher - sixth through eighth grade - and she is one of the best teachers I've ever had.

Bellamy Young

When I was 3, my mom sent in a video of me singing George Strait to 'America's Funniest Home Videos.'

Austin Mahone

My mom is the recycling Nazi, and I always bring a bag to the grocery store.

Jane Levy

I don't know that I have any role models now that are fixed. Definitely my mom - she's the coolest. She's worked really hard her whole life and I just think she's got a great attitude. Moms just know so much it's so silly.

Larisa Oleynik

My mom was incredibly supportive when she found out that I wanted to be an actress, and that certainly made things easier and more fun.

Morena Baccarin

I come from a short fiction background, and my mom is a poet, so I've always read poetry; I've always had a lot of different influences both linguistically and musically.

Lorde

I'd never really babysat. I feel like I'm Blair, or 'Gossip

Girl.' A teenager, basically - and now suddenly I'm a mom?

Cecily von Ziegesar

I took a long period off to be a mom.

Mia Farrow

Before I was a mom I used to think that parents who worried about their kids watching MTV were just clueless. Now that I'm a mom, I see what the fuss was all about!

Martha Quinn

When I first came out, I was a film student, and my mom sewed clothes. I was already doing a million things then, whatever it took to survive. If I had to braid someone's hair to get one pound for my lunch money, that's what I did.

M.I.A.

My mom played tennis for, like, six hours a day and went to college on a tennis scholarship, because that was the way she could go to school. So they instilled in me the idea that you have to work hard for the things you want in life and never complain.

Dakota Fanning

I have lots of records, quite a collection, actually, that I stole from my mom. I have the original 'Thriller' album and I have a really great 'Elton John's Greatest Hits,' and I also have a N.E.R.D. album. Records sound more original. They have more edge.

Elisha Cuthbert

On my best days, I fancy myself a combination of Dad's persistence/patience and Mom's toughness/skepticism.

David Einhorn

My mom's a Catholic, and my dad's a Jew, and they didn't want anything to do with anything.

Isabelle Huppert

So much of our lives are defined by habit or what the guy next to us is doing, never wondering and knowing who and what we support with our actions, from the detergent Mom always used, to my favorite dish I make... A lot of my life is unexamined habit.

Kristin Bauer van Straten

I feel like I've been very smart in the way that I carry myself and treat myself. I feel like my mom was a big part of that just because she's always let us make our own decisions, and we've known very much about the mistakes and the dangers already of whatever this Hollywood life may be.

Evan Ross

www.ingramcontent.com/pod-product-compliance
Lightning Source LLC
Chambersburg PA
CBHW070638290526
45790CB00001B/133